To: _____

From: _____

The Spirit of Christmas

Books by Cynthia Ruchti

Facing the Dawn

The Spirit of Christmas

Restoring Christmas

An Endless Christmas

The Spirit of Christmas

DISCOVERING HIS PRESENCE THROUGHOUT THE ADVENT SEASON

CYNTHIA RUCHTI

Chosen

a division of Baker Publishing Group
Minneapolis, Minnesota

Published by Chosen Books
Minneapolis, Minnesota
ChosenBooks.com

Chosen Books is a division of
Baker Publishing Group, Grand Rapids, Michigan

Printed in the United States of America

ISBN 9780800772802 (paper)
ISBN 9781493452255 (ebook)

Library of Congress Cataloging-in-Publication Control Number: 2025002723

Cover design by Peter Gloege, Look Design Studio

Published in association with Books & Such Literary Management, BooksAndSuch.com.

Baker Publishing Group publications use paper produced from sustainable forestry practices and postconsumer waste whenever possible.

25   26   27   28   29   30   31   7   6   5   4   3   2   1

*To the One who hovers
over and breathes within us
this Advent season and always.*

This Advent season, we can continue to train
our focus on unwashed shepherds
and an uncomfortable birthing center,
or we can turn our attention to watch for
the not-so-hidden evidence
of the presence of the Spirit.

INTRODUCTION

The spirits of Christmas Past, Present, and Future gave Scrooge the worst case of insomnia in *A Christmas Carol*. But the Spirit of Christmas is not a Dickens concept. The Spirit of the living God has forever been an integral part of the Savior's birth story we celebrate at Christmas, since long before the holy babe was conceived.

We haven't always noticed. We've focused on tattered shepherds and loud-mouthed angels. We've focused on a silent stable, road-weary wise men and curious stars, or a wide-eyed young mom and her stymied fiancé.

But the Spirit was there. The Bible tells us He hovered over waters and chaos prior to God the Father's words that gave birth to beginnings. And He hovers over every page of the Christmas story.

This Advent season, we can continue to train our focus on unwashed shepherds and an uncomfortable birthing center, or we can turn our attention to watch for the not-so-hidden evidence of the presence of the Spirit.

On the spaces provided, feel free to record your impressions of those Spirit-sightings as we walk through this evidence together. Included in the back of the book are additional resources, links to accompanying music, and ten family Christmas activities to help you make room for the Spirit.

What you discover may form a new tradition for you and your family—a Christmas seek-and-find.

The Christmas Story Started in a Garden

Now the earth was formless and empty, darkness was over the surface of the deep, and the Spirit of God was hovering over the waters.

Genesis 1:2

*T*ell me the Christmas story, Grandpa."

When has a request like that ever been answered with a cleared throat and the words "Way back before there was day and night, sun and moon, plants and animals, way before people existed, the Spirit of God hovered over the waters, the chaos, the nothingness"?

The child interrupts, tempering her rising frustration. "Grandpa, tell me about the reindeer and the elves and the candy canes."

"That's not the real Christmas story."

"Then tell me the *real* one, with the baby in the hay and 'no room in the inn' and angels singing 'Go Tell It on the Mountain.' There's no Spirit in that story."

"Oh, but there is. And that makes it all the more amazing."

• • •

Grandpa was right. The Christmas story we cherish, the one we've built a whole season around, the one we celebrate with candlelight services and charcuterie boards, with sacrificial giving (or overspending) and aromas that have become treasured memories—sugar cookies, hot cider, cinnamon, glazed ham or roast turkey or both—is a Holy Spirit story.

He was there from the beginning. It started in a garden.

Like searching for family origins, we can trace the presence of the Holy Spirit to a time before Eden was a reality—fully documented in the book of Genesis. The Spirit hovered over the Creation scene, stirring the waters as He often does, directing the wind, breathing life into bird and lizard lungs and Adam's lungs. God said, "Let us make mankind in *our* image" (Genesis 1:26, emphasis added). So they—Father, Son, and Holy Spirit—did.

The first time the Spirit was grieved also took place in the Garden, when sin entered the scene, introducing rot, decay, and death into the newly formed, perfect world. This act also introduced our obvious need for a Savior.

They say the first crime recorded in the Bible was murder—Cain's murder of Abel. But wasn't the first crime stealing? Robbery? God clearly informed Adam and Eve that everything else in the Garden was free for them to eat (see Genesis 2:16–17). He also clearly said, "This tree is mine. No trespassing. Do not take and eat from this one, specific tree."

But with unimaginable abundance around them, Adam and Eve ignored what had been the only existing edict, stole God's property (I'd forgotten about the trespassing part until just now. You, too?), poisoned the atmosphere that had not known disease until that moment, and hacked into the system to rewire our DNA for pain, addiction, misplaced affections, relationship conflict, and the big one—death.

How many life sentences could be piled on top of one another?

But the Father, the Son, and the Holy Spirit loved what they'd created together. With the pronouncement of humanity's sentence recorded in Genesis 3, they also shared the first hint that a Redeemer would come to defeat the enemy who had defeated God's children.

Adam and Eve didn't know they wouldn't live to see that Redeemer, Jesus, arrive as a babe. What kind of therapy would they have needed if they'd been told it would be (by some accounts) four thousand years before anyone worthy of the task would step in to shoulder their sentence? The indictment their children and grandchildren and great-great-(plus an estimated 131 more greats) grandchildren had been subject to since Eve's hand touched a fruit's velvety skin? The two broken people in the first Garden likely told each other, "Just wait. Help is coming."

And thus was born the first cry of "How long?"

Consider this. In the New Testament, we're told that the velvety, God-given fruit of the Holy Spirit—evidence that the Holy Spirit is at work within us—is characterized by love, joy, peace, *patience* . . . (see Galatians 5:22–23).

The connection between the Holy Spirit and patience began in the Garden. He knew the Redeemer would eventually come, bringing what we now call Christmas.

For millennia—grieved but hopeful and always hovering—the Spirit continued to whisper, *Patience. Wait with hope.*

◆ PONDERINGS ◆

How far back can you trace your ancestors? How many generations?

How far back can you trace your family's *faith* history?

This Christmas, will your family be the first in your line to honor the presence of the Holy Spirit woven throughout the Christmas story, or are you carrying on a cherished tradition of recognizing He's been there all along?

What have you been longing for, praying for, waiting for? In the stillness of this moment, can you hear the Spirit whisper, *Wait with hope?*

◆ ADVENT PRAYER ◆

Spirit of the living God, fall fresh on me
as I move through these days
anticipating Christmas,
noticing and celebrating You.
Amen.

Isaiah's Conversation with the Spirit

For unto us a Child is born.

Isaiah 9:6 NKJV

Has your family started planning meals for your holiday get-togethers? If a charcuterie board is somewhere in your planning, you're so on-trend. Are your holidays meals largely traditional—same stuffing or dressing recipe served in the same bowl Great-Grandma used? Same veggie sides? Same array of pies—pumpkin for Mom and pecan for Dad and chocolate silk for the kids?

After all that meal prep, inevitably someone shows up and announces, "I'm on a juice cleanse this week," or "Sorry. I just ate. I'll have a glass of water, please. No ice."

Three hundred years ago, a great deal of thought was put into meals for a man who was so laser-focused on his work that for almost three weeks he refused everything prepared for him. He barely slept. Those who brought him food returned many hours later to find it untouched. Day after day.

The task with which the man was so obsessed? Committing to paper what the Holy Spirit was moving him to pen, a masterpiece we now know as Handel's *Messiah*. The motivation that kept George Frideric Handel up at night—furiously scribbling so he didn't miss any nuance—was rooted in what had kept Isaiah the prophet up all night 2,400 years earlier—a voice from heaven speaking into the darkness:

> For unto us a Child is born,
> Unto us a Son is given;
> And the government will be upon His shoulder.
> And His name will be called
> Wonderful, Counselor, Mighty God,
> Everlasting Father, Prince of Peace.
>
> Isaiah 9:6 NKJV

A performance of Handel's *Messiah*, with the above Scripture verse among the lyrics, may well be part of your Advent or Christmas traditions. A community or church choir concert. Or a high school choral concert.

In our small town in the Midwest, the final song of the annual high school Christmas concert was always a hold-your-breath, wait-for-it, now-I'm-in-the-Christmas-spirit moment.

The finale began with an invitation from the choral director to the audience. Any past choir members, no matter how long ago they'd graduated, were invited to join the freshmen, sophomores, juniors, and seniors on the risers. Although students offered to share their music folders, most of the adults didn't need the prop.

The words and passion of Handel's *Messiah* had followed them after graduation and lived in their memories. The "Hallelujah" chorus rang out with both young and mature voices forming a soul-stirring blend of rejoicing that never failed to move the concertgoers.

The piece united young and old in our public high school. It impressed mechanics and bank presidents, grocery clerks and stylists, doctors and military veterans, and teachers who told others to "watch your language" regarding any discussion related to faith, God, Jesus, or the Bible. It was an oratorio originally composed for an Easter performance (Christ's resurrection as the finale), not Christmas.

The finale—final stamp—of the concert? "And He shall reign forever and ever. King of kings and Lord of lords. Forever. And ever. And ever. And ever. And ever . . . Hal-le-lu-jah!"

Atheist, agnostic, Christ follower, *passionate* Christ follower—all who have ever joined that chorus have confessed with their mouths that Jesus is Lord.

Why would that have been allowed? Because Handel's *Messiah* is considered a work of musical art . . . as is everything the Spirit of God touches.

We're told the lyrics of the *Messiah* were taken from the books of Isaiah, Haggai, Malachi, Luke, Zechariah, Matthew, John, Psalms, Lamentations, Romans, Revelation, Job, and 1 Corinthians. I have intentionally kept these mentions beyond the confines of alphabetical or chronological order. As Handel's *Messiah* was written, the composer drew from whichever part of Scripture spoke to that musical moment.

The thrilling connections make me want to add, as the psalmists often did, *SELAH* (which from the Hebrew is often translated "pause and reflect").

Where do you turn when you or your family is interested in taking a look at the Christmas story, the story of Jesus's birth? The second chapter of Luke? It's the go-to.

Those few verses provide only part of the narrative, though. As George Frideric Handel did, we can find elements scattered like delicious charcuterie board bread crumbs—or pita scraps—leading us to the destination of Jesus. And who scattered the crumbs? The Holy Spirit.

Let's focus on the Isaiah portion of the story as we observe the presence of the Holy Spirit throughout every layer of Advent, the same that Handel explored when composing "For unto us a child is born."[1]

We might assume the prophet Isaiah was unaware how wide-reaching his message would be. He would not have imagined that his words would find their way into the canon of Scripture, the body of writing we know as the Bible. It's hard to imagine the prophet could have predicted anyone would put his words to music that would become an iconic December song to help usher in the holiday season for so many people over the centuries. Or that you may have taken the opportunity to listen to it a few minutes ago.

God's Word tells us that two of the Holy Spirit's assignments are to offer comfort and hope (see John 14:26; 16:7; Romans 15:13). It's hard to comprehend how many people have taken comfort and drawn hope from these potent and stirring words since they were breathed into the atmosphere in ages past:

> And His name will be called
> Wonderful, Counselor, Mighty God,
> Everlasting Father, Prince of Peace.

If you're like me, the Spirit within roars to life when a chorale or orchestra reaches the heavily accented "Wonderful!" in Handel's version.

This "unto us is born" child, this Jesus Christ.

Predicted, promised, prophesied.

The short passage is so memorable it comes to mind without much prompting. Lingering there (*selah*) can reveal so much about the Promised One. The Christ child, the Son, who is also called Mighty God. The Son who is known as Everlasting Father.

Revelation floods us with a reminder that Father, Son, and Holy Spirit are one. What is true about God the Father is true about the Son and about the Holy Spirit.

Many have wondered why the prophet Isaiah used words best translated "is born." It hadn't happened yet. Some scholars say the grammatical tense Isaiah uses is not the present perfect tense most graduates are quick to leave behind when they finish their final English class.

It is instead a *prophetic* perfect tense literary technique, viewing something yet to happen with the surety as if it has been already accomplished.

Isaiah, the same prophet, tells us that the Son of God *was* wounded for our transgressions, although that action would not happen until long into the future (see Isaiah 53:5).

When the ancient prophet claimed that "unto us a Child is born," he'd been given—by insight from the Holy Spirit—the words and confidence for an action that would not be fulfilled for seven hundred years. And yet, because of God's faithfulness and unchanging nature, for Isaiah and those who listened to him, it was as good as done . . . until the moment it *was* done.

The culture in which Isaiah lived was desperate for a wise and trustworthy counselor, desperate for assurance, desperate for peace. The people were divided, held captive, resorting to ransom, with distress and darkness and fear part of their everyday existence.

But that prophetic perfect tense (don't stress, not on the test) promise flowed from Isaiah's mouth—"For unto us a Child is born" (Isaiah 9:6 NKJV).

Isaiah wouldn't have known that seven hundred years would pass before the birth of Jesus and the fulfillment of that prophecy. We—included in the *us* of "unto us"—look behind us more than two thousand years. By now, humanity has talked about that child almost three times as long as Isaiah's prophecy was old before it came to pass.

Catch the role of the Spirit when, a couple of chapters later in Isaiah, the prophet is inspired to say, "A shoot will come up from the stump of Jesse [from David's family tree]; from his roots a Branch will bear fruit. The *Spirit* of the LORD will rest on him—the *Spirit* of wisdom and of understanding, the *Spirit* of counsel and of might, the *Spirit* of the knowledge and fear of the LORD—and he will delight in the fear of the LORD" (Isaiah 11:1–3, emphasis added).

Was Isaiah convinced the Holy Spirit flows freely through the ancient and yet ever-new story of the Christ child?

Forever and ever, and ever, and ever . . . hallelujah!

◆ PONDERINGS ◆

What's your or your family's favorite Christmas song? A carol? A hymn?

Create a playlist of only your favorites, weeding out the reindeer and snowflakes and focusing on the impact of the birth of the Christ child, the gift of the Father, or the presence of the Spirit.

◆ ADVENT PRAYER ◆

*Spirit of God, help us notice the "crumbs" You left
throughout the Word that point so clearly
to the truth on which we rest our faith.
Amen.*

Holy Spirit Nudges
AT CHRISTMAS

Most of us recognize when we're being prompted to go out of our way to bless someone, to serve or give or meet a need. We may not have always recognized it, though, as a nudge from the Holy Spirit.

This Advent season, consider how He may be prompting you to do the outrageous. Even with the cost of the meal more like a down payment on a house, consider forfeiting your own lavish Christmas dinner in favor of frozen pizza for Christmas Day. Offer your turkey or ham and trimmings to a needy family.

Immanuel, God with Us . . . God Within Us

"The virgin will conceive and give birth to a son, and they will call him Immanuel" (which means "God with us").

Matthew 1:23

*I*s a trip to the craft or hobby store part of your routine when preparing your home for the holidays? If so, you may wrestle with a spelling dilemma. A wreath in one aisle sports a gold-edged ribbon with the name Emmanuel. In the next aisle, a piece of antique-looking decoupage-able sheet music is titled "Immanuel."

Clearance-bin treasures reveal a rustic tin sign with a small boo-boo in the corner. It is easy to disguise with a sprig of holly, and the price is more than fair. But will you have to fight off the grammar nerds if it hangs in your home? The wording is "Emanuel—God with us." What happened to the other *M*?

Come to think of it, your neighborhood boasts an Immanuel Lutheran, an Emanuel Baptist, and an Emmanuel Church of the Holiness of the Almighty God Eternal Joy assembly. Those church-naming teams must have undergone quite the spelling debate before settling on their majority-rules choice.

Or is there another explanation? And why would it matter, if it does?

In the Old Testament, whose historical records, prophecy, and poetry were written in Hebrew, the name is Immanuel from the Hebrew and Aramaic *Immanu* (with us) + *El* (God). In the New Testament, recorded in Greek—the written language of the day—the name emphasizes the purpose of the word *Emmanouel*, shortened to Emmanuel in most translations. In essence, one translates the pronunciation. The other translates the meaning.[1]

The amazement for us, though, is that Immanuel of 2,700 years ago and Emmanuel of about 2,000 years ago is Immanuel/ Emmanuel/Emanuel of today—Jesus, God-with-us. We don't take it lightly that the God-with-us promised in Isaiah 7:14 is the God-with-us fulfilled in Jesus of the Matthew record in the New Testament and the God-with-us (present tense) through the Holy Spirit with—as in *within*—us now.

Isaiah 7:14 notes the prophetic words, "Therefore the Lord himself will give you a sign: The virgin will conceive and give birth to a son, and will call him Immanuel."

Matthew 1:22 reveals a personal comment in the middle of Joseph's dream about the child his betrothed, Mary, is carrying. The angel of the Lord assures Joseph that this is God's plan, that the child is to be called Jesus "because he will save his people from their sins" (Matthew 1:21). Matthew's comment is this: "All this took place to fulfill what the Lord has said through the prophet: 'The virgin will conceive and give birth to a son, and they will call him Immanuel' (which means 'God with us')" (Matthew 1:22–23).

Matthew wanted no one to misunderstand. The child Isaiah called Immanuel is the child the Holy Spirit implanted in Mary, the Jesus whom Matthew proclaimed as the prophecy's fulfillment.

The ancient Israelites heard Isaiah's prophecy and wondered what it could mean.

Early New Testament–era believers knew Jesus as God with (among) them. There in the flesh beside them, walking the roads they walked, eating with them, speaking with them, healing their diseases and heartaches, telling stories that both captivated and confused them. He was with them in human form . . . for a time. Spoiler alert: He dies young.

We are the generations blessed to know a "with" deeper than even the disciples—His closest followers—could begin to experience before Jesus returned to the right hand of His Father. We know this Immanuel/Emmanuel within.

Where is the Holy Spirit in the Christmas story? He is the Immanuel who never leaves, the one Jesus in the flesh remarkably described as better than His presence with those with whom He walked and talked. Better? Could Jesus have misspoken?

No. He never chose the wrong word. He *is* the Word (see John 1).

He specifically selected the word *better* or *for your benefit, to your advantage*, as the Greek and other Bible translations express it. What could be better than being in the room where it happens, standing so near Jesus that the disciples could see beads of sweat on His brow, His squint against the midday sun, hear from His own ears the around-the-campfire story of His birth, first told to Him by His mother?

Better?

It may not seem like a typical Advent Scripture passage, but consider rereading Jesus's heartfelt words to His closest followers in the days before His physical presence left them. John chapters 14–16 can provide a far more beautiful backdrop than any mantel decoration or wreath on the door as the Christmas celebration approaches.

In essence, Jesus is encouraging us not to get spiritually stuck in the Bethlehem stable and not to rest our faith on His birth alone. We're not to stay rooted in only what He did while on earth. That's nearsighted. He's urging His followers—us—not to cling to the image of our Savior on the cross, or of the empty cross, or even of the empty tomb.

Each of those events is important. They are vital components of our understanding of God and His plan and of Jesus and His sacrificial life, death, and resurrection.

Jesus carefully chose His words when telling His followers that something even more spectacular, better, fuller, and more advantageous was on the horizon for them that would serve as a promise for all of us since that moment.

His coming to earth brought hope. His leaving the earth offered us the opportunity to be comforted more fully, to be taught more than He had time to teach in person, and to reach more than He could reach on foot.

What a stirring concept! Jesus had more to tell us and was eager for the season in which, although He was returning to His Father, we could have the advantage of the Holy Spirit within us, ever-present.

Where is the Holy Spirit in the nativity scene at church? He is in those who observe it. Where is He in the songs we cherish? In the breath of our voices. Where is He in gift exchanges? In us, spurred by His generosity in giving and His humility in asking nothing in return.

Where will we find the Holy Spirit in our Advent preparations? In the wisdom of decisions, the counsel of ways to bless others, the stirring in our hearts that celebrates a story started long ago with captivating chapters that include this Immanuel, this Emmanuel, residing within us.

Inseparable presence.

Unspeakable peace.

◆ PONDERINGS ◆

Take a moment to look up companion verses Isaiah 7:14 and Matthew 1:23 in the Bible you use most often. Note that the KJV uses Emmanuel. The NKJV, NASB, NLT, HCSB, and NIV, among others, use the Immanuel spelling. No matter the version, it's the same God-with-us. How does that have an impact on your appreciation of the nearness of God?

◆ ADVENT PRAYER ◆

*Holy Spirit, we recognize that Your presence within
changes how we view all the external elements
that herald Christ's coming as a babe.
Give us clear vision to see
where we may have missed You in years past.
We look to You as our Comfort, Guide, Protector,
Convincer, and Revealer of the heart of God the Father,
as Jesus promised.
Soften our hearts to the story long-told.
May we see Christmas as You see it,
from Your divine and indwelling perspective.
Amen.*

O Significant Town of Bethlehem

"But you, Bethlehem Ephrathah, though you are small among the clans of Judah, out of you will come for me one who will be ruler over Israel, whose origins are from of old, from ancient times."

Micah 5:2

My father spent Christmas in an orphanage one year. He and his Marine buddies visited an orphanage near where they were stationed. I was a babe in arms in the heart of the United States living with my mother and grandparents until he returned from his military stint—if he returned. That December, I would have been eleven months old. I can't imagine my mother's aching preparation, the separation from her husband and not-yet-toddling child in her care serving as raw reminders that the Advent season is not jingly bells and crowded dining-room tables for everyone.

And Daddy? I can't imagine approaching Christmas from that perspective—so many miles from home, so much danger close at hand, so far from anything familiar, traditional, safe.

One of my treasured possessions is a photograph of Dad in his Marine fatigues distributing candy and small gifts to eager children in that orphanage halfway around the world. In another picture, he's holding a little fatherless girl not much older than I would have been at the time. He hugged and brought joy to a child near him when he couldn't wrap his arms around his own.

The prophets who foretold Christ's coming to earth as a babe were distant in both miles and years from the realization of what they proclaimed. I imagine they often didn't know any more details than what had been spoken to them by the Spirit. For the prophet Micah, that must have been especially true.

It is from Micah 5:2 that we learn the birthplace of the centuries-into-the-future King with a capital *K*—Bethlehem. From the New King James Version:

> "But you, Bethlehem Ephrathah,
> Though you are little among the thousands of Judah,
> Yet out of you shall come forth to Me
> The One to be Ruler in Israel,
> Whose goings forth are from of old,
> From everlasting."

Expanded to take in the perspective added in verse 3 in *The Message* version:

> But you, Bethlehem, David's country,
>   the runt of the litter—
> From you will come the leader
>   who will shepherd-rule Israel.
> He'll be no upstart, no pretender.
>   His family tree is ancient and distinguished.
> Meanwhile, Israel will be in foster homes
>   until the birth pangs are over and the child is born.

The poetry of that creative interpretation of the Micah prophecy helps point us to what some people find surprising—the Son of God was born in a small and humble town. To those of us who have studied and appreciated the way Jesus conducted Himself in life and ministry, it makes sense. Humility marked everything He did.

O humble, little town of Bethlehem!

Or should we be singing, "O significant town of Bethlehem"? The rhythm is harder to dance to, but the meaning becomes clear when we see the threads of ancient days connecting and intersecting at Bethlehem.

Bethlehem is first mentioned in Scripture in the book of Genesis. It was the place nearest where Jacob laid his beloved Rachel to rest when she died (see Genesis 35:19).

In the fields on the outskirts of Bethlehem, Ruth met Boaz, who served as a kinsman redeemer in her time of hardship and distress (see Ruth 2). From their marriage union, a child was born—Obed. Obed grew to father Jesse (see Ruth 4). Jesse was the father of many sons, one of them the boy who would become King David.

We know from biblical history that David's family lived in and around Bethlehem and that David considered Bethlehem his cherished hometown. The lineage hadn't traveled far from the place where God had met the displaced refugee Ruth and provided a redeemer in Boaz.

If we trace the family tree for more generations, we intersect with Bethlehem again, not as Jesus's family's hometown—which was Nazareth. The intersection was a symbol of both political upheaval and oppression. Tax time equaled census-taking to make sure no one was overlooked or escaped paying. And Bethlehem was the central location to which all surrounding residents reported for the census.

If the expectant Mary had her preferences, she would have no doubt wanted the baby to be born close to home in Nazareth with her mother or female cousins nearby to help. But Mary knew the ancient writings and may not have been surprised at all that her birth pangs began on the road to Bethlehem. The prophet Micah had heard the whispers of the Holy Spirit hundreds of years earlier proclaiming the child we now know as Jesus would be born in that specific town of Bethlehem.

For those who might wonder if God is truly in the details, it's fascinating to note that between Abraham and the rule of David is fourteen generations. From David to the Babylonian exile is fourteen generations. From the exile and silence from heaven to the birth of Christ is fourteen generations.

Bethlehem's mention in the Old and New Testaments is no accident or coincidence. This "little town" appears fifty times in the Bible. And it's no wonder. Its very name—House of Bread (from the Hebrew *beth* and *lechem*) is referenced again when Jesus is revealed as the Bread of Life.[1] O significant town of Bethlehem!

I think about the prophet Micah when I glance at the small, insignificant (some might say) photograph on my desk—my daddy smiling and holding a child who represented the one waiting for him in the future. The Holy Spirit moved on Micah to report to all who would listen about a child waiting for them in *their* future. Of all the villages and cities, Bethlehem was spoken by name as that child's birthplace, a town that has always represented birth, burial, and redemption.

This Advent, may we be the kind of people to whom the Spirit of God can whisper holy comfort like that.

◆ PONDERINGS ◆

In the Additional Resources portion at the end of this book, you'll find a link to an orchestral version of "O Little Town of Bethlehem." As you listen, consider how large a place in human history is occupied by a small, insignificant town and how that town has so sweet a place in our hearts.

◆ ADVENT PRAYER ◆

*Holy Spirit, may we, like Micah
and others before and since,
listen intently for Your voice,
believe what You tell us,
and use every opportunity
to bring hope to others
with what we hear from You.
Amen.*

Holy Spirit Nudges
AT CHRISTMAS

The Holy Spirit is a gift giver, as we're told often in Scripture. He's creative with widely varied gifts. Who around you will be without a gift this Christmas unless you step in? A single mom? Or a single dad? An older person whose family members live too far away to visit at Christmas? Someone whose job keeps them working through the holidays? Consider purchasing a meaningful but inexpensive gift and including a printed copy of the characteristics of the Holy Spirit listed in Day 18.

The Spirit Loves Babies

Both of them were righteous in the sight of God, observing all the Lord's commands and decrees blamelessly. But they were childless because Elizabeth was not able to conceive, and they were both very old.

Luke 1:6–7

The miracles of the Advent story continue to mount. Evidence of the presence of the Spirit of God grows, too, as we draw closer to the date artificially set for us to commemorate the birth of Christ.

One of the hurdles in understanding the circumstances of what we call the Christmas story in the Bible is how vastly different our culture is from what society looked like then.

How long has it been since you called your aunt and uncle or cousin? Me, too. I'll make myself a note. Maybe text them.

Send them an email to say, "I'm thinking of you." Video-call to catch up.

Any of those options are doable—and perhaps a good Advent activity, especially for those you won't see during the holidays.

But those were not options available in biblical times. Messages were sent primarily through messengers who traveled on foot, by wagon, or on horseback. Sometimes messages were held in reserve until a tradesperson or friend was traveling near the area where relatives lived.

So it's no surprise that what was happening at Zechariah and Elizabeth's home couldn't be communicated by a quick call from Mary or Mary's mother. Some scholars say Elizabeth was Mary's cousin. Some say she was Mary's maternal aunt. But no matter the family connection, they would not have reason or ability for daily communication because of the distance of about one hundred miles between Nazareth and Ain Karim, which was in the hill country. The two women were related, but they likely did not see each other often.

Elizabeth and Zechariah's story in the Bible starts in Luke 1 with a bit about their heritage, then two consecutive sentences that both hint at why their story is included in Luke's account of everything-that-happened-worth-telling and create a disconnect in some readers' minds.

"Both of them were righteous in the sight of God, observing all the Lord's commands and decrees blamelessly. But they were childless because Elizabeth was not able to conceive, and they were both very old" (Luke 1:6–7).

Righteous, blameless . . . and barren.

They were doing all the right things, obeying the Lord faithfully, but unable to enjoy the most precious of life's joys—children—and the legacy they would maintain for their family lines.

The Bible states that it wasn't Zechariah but Elizabeth who couldn't conceive. Thanks for mentioning that detail, Luke. And as if that weren't enough, they were both not just aging but "very old." Her clock had stopped ticking long ago.

If their story starts that way, readers will know it doesn't end that way. Thanks for giving away the plot, Luke. But we're glad you did.

Verses 13–15 provide a glimpse of what's to come. Zechariah is minding his own business, or rather God's business, serving in the temple as was his duty, burning incense while the people outside prayed. An angel of the Lord appeared and, as angels often do, said:

"Do not be afraid, Zechariah; your prayer has been heard. Your wife Elizabeth will bear you a son, and you are to call him John. He will be a joy and delight to you, and many will rejoice because of his birth, for he will be great in the sight of the Lord. He is never to take wine or other fermented drink, and he will be filled with the Holy Spirit even before he is born."

Luke 1:13–15

In the middle of the prayer meeting, an angel appeared to answer Zechariah's prayer. Zechariah's response? Like others before him, Zechariah doubted God could make that happen.

These weren't his words, but in our day, we might have said, "You've got to be kidding! We signed up for Medicare years ago!"

The angel (Gabriel, it turns out—keep that name in mind for future reference) was probably one cup of coffee shy of his minimum for the day or had heard one too many whiners who doubted the God for whom nothing is impossible. He declared to Zechariah, "Okay, now you can be afraid." Or words to that effect. "I have been sent to speak to you and to tell you this good news. And now you will be silent and not able to speak until the day this happens, because you did not believe my words, which will come true at their appointed time" (Luke 1:19–20).

There's more to the story. We know the baby, John, who will be born despite Zechariah's doubts, is the man we know as John the Baptizer, the preacher who paved the way for the coming of Jesus, although we can peek behind the scenes and know that at the time Gabe spoke to Zechariah—and promised that a year later he'd be getting up in the middle of the night with a baby named John—Mary wasn't pregnant.

God had to first answer a decades-long prayer for Zechariah and Elizabeth—those two in particular—before He could reveal that the Messiah would be born soon after.

This, though, is what merits our particular attention during this Advent season when we are focusing on the search-and-find for where the Holy Spirit shows up in the Christmas story. What was predicted about baby John? He would be filled with the Spirit even before he was born!

The Spirit was a gift from God for holy purposes, and He would function as a comforter, guide, shield, protector, counselor, and teacher for John. John would have reason to depend on the Holy Spirit his entire life. Spoiler alert: He, too, dies young.

God is very patient with us humans. He slides clues and hints between the lines to help us connect the dots. Keep your eyes open for evidence that the Spirit inhabited John while he was still in the womb of a woman too old to have babies.

As we transition into the next act of their scenes in the Christmas story, we find Zechariah unable to speak and Elizabeth with her first taste of morning sickness. If Zechariah hadn't been already mute, that would have been enough to render him speechless.

It's a good thing the Holy Spirit loves babies.

◆ PONDERINGS ◆

Spend time thinking about how many babies were announced by a messenger or directly through the Holy Spirit in the Bible. Abraham was told he would father many children (see Genesis 17:4–6) though he had none at the time and was already aged. Hannah was told Samuel would be born (see 1 Samuel 1:17–18) even though she'd been barren her whole marriage. Zechariah heard the Holy Spirit through an angel declare that John would be born to his elderly wife (see Luke 1:13). Mary was told about Jesus (see Luke 1:31).

What does it stir in you when you consider how prolific the examples are of the Holy Spirit's work in announcing babies?

◆ ADVENT PRAYER ◆

How like You, Lord God Almighty,
to choose to work through
the most helpless and dependent
of us—a child.
How grateful we are that You did!
And how awe-inspiring it is
that the Holy Spirit
cherished the task
of making the announcements!
Amen.

Zechariah's Forfeit to the Spirit

"And now you will be silent and not able to speak until the day this happens, because you did not believe my words, which will come true at their appointed time."

Luke 1:20

Silenced, humbled because of his doubts, Zechariah spent the entire nine months with only one person he could really talk to—the Holy Spirit.

He could write and make hand gestures for a cup of water or a second helping of lamb stew. But conversations? All his conversations that whole time were deep in his soul as he listened to and responded to the Spirit, as he adjusted his thinking to realize God means what He says.

Zechariah, no doubt, silently apologized for doubting. But it may have gone much deeper than that. He had been faithful to pray but, like us too often, he either didn't trust that God could or would answer his prayer, or didn't like the *way* God chose to answer.

It's not hard to imagine that he had many questions for the Holy Spirit. *What did God the Father mean about my son bringing back many of our people to worship the true God? My son? How could my son prepare the way for the Lord? That's what the angel said. But how? What will that require of us as parents? Are we to send him to special training?*

Zechariah couldn't even tell the story of what had happened to him in the angel encounter without scribbling fragments of it on a tablet. Did he have to rely on the Hebrew version of exclamation points to underscore the angel's tone of voice?

The Bible says he stayed at the temple and fulfilled his duties. He didn't return immediately to Elizabeth, the one person who might have understood his makeshift sign language. Elizabeth might have heard rumors about her husband turning suddenly mute during his priestly responsibilities. What must she have thought when he came home, his heart full of what he could not express?

Was he able to communicate enough for her to know that when she started craving cinnamon cakes and couldn't look at a piece of raw meat she was not imagining those things? Could he reassure her that she wasn't facing death but carrying new life?

Her aching-to-be-a-mother heart knew. She also knew without a word from her husband that God had done this.

For the first five months, Elizabeth remained in seclusion. Bible scholars and wannabe scholars are widely divided on why she would stay out of sight, out of the public eye. It wouldn't have been a cultural norm. It may have been that she was tending this pregnancy carefully, perhaps from a long history of failed attempts or miscarriages, although the Bible specifically says she couldn't conceive, not that she couldn't carry a child to term. She would not have known that an angel was soon to visit Mary. We just know that she wanted to keep quiet about her pregnancy until then.

Zechariah's vision said nothing about how soon the Lord—for whom his son, John, was to prepare the way—would arrive. Was it when John was still an infant, a teen, a grown man? Nothing in the vision informed them that Mary would even be involved.

That leaves a couple of more believable options as we consider the role Zechariah and Elizabeth play in our Advent preparations and the Christmas story. Elizabeth may have decided to join Zechariah in his enforced "vow of silence" to ponder and quietly consider what God had done on their behalf. She may have heard from the Holy Spirit in her own prayer times and was obeying a directive of which we're not aware.

It appears to have been a holy, sacred time for both of them—their social disgrace in the process of being removed, a baby on the way, the promise that Zechariah would speak again, but that their God was serious about being believed.

Elizabeth eventually began to feel better. Her belly began to swell with life. She may have felt small flutters. But the Holy Spirit was about to appear on the scene in a far-beyond-flutter way.

◆ PONDERINGS ◆

What's the last thing that rendered you speechless? Was it awe of what the Holy Spirit can do that caused it? Was it a loss for words? Did you lean into the promises that were fulfilled in Jesus in that moment?

◆ ADVENT PRAYER ◆

May the words of my mouth
or the silence of my awe
give You glory this day
and every day.
Amen.

The Night Visitor

"Greetings, you who are highly favored!"

Luke 1:28

Do you remember Gabe, or rather Gabriel, the angel who startled Zechariah and showed him a divine positive pregnancy test for his geriatric wife, Elizabeth?

In Elizabeth's sixth month of pregnancy, God said to the angel, "Dude, I have another mission for you." (That's from a not-yet-published *unauthorized* version of God's Holy Word.) Gabriel was dispensed to visit a young woman, many believe as young as fourteen years old, who lived in a little town called Nazareth. His message? Similar to the one Gabe shared with Zechariah, but with a twist.

He started his message with the traditional angelic intro: "Fear not." Actually, that came later. First the angel said, "Greetings."

Christmas hadn't been invented yet, or it might have been "Pre-Christmas greetings to you!"

When we draw close to the Word of God, we are far more likely to spot the presence of the Holy Spirit in any circumstance. Watch this instance unfold so beautifully that it takes our breath away.

Gabriel said, "Greetings, you who are highly favored! The Lord is with you" (verse 28).

It's no surprise Mary "wondered what kind of greeting this might be" (verse 29). She was so troubled that the angel had to repeat himself, this time beginning with, "Do not be afraid, Mary; you have found favor with God" (verse 30).

Both Zechariah and Mary were called by name. The angelic messages were specifically meant for those two individuals. "Do not be afraid, Zechariah." Then a little more than six months later, "Do not be afraid, Mary." The personalization of these two angel visits and the common ground in the messages stir within the careful observer great appreciation for how tenderly and intentionally both were handled.

It's as if Gabriel held another pregnancy test in his hand. In Mary's case, though, the angel confidently said, "You will conceive and give birth to a son, and you are to call him Jesus. He will be great" (Luke 1:31–32). To this point, it's almost a duplication of the pattern regarding the pending birth of Zechariah's son, John, except for the name thing.

What must Mary have thought when the angel's next words to her were "and [He] will be called the Son of the Most High" (verse 32)? Many of us would ask to see the angel's navigation app. "Huh. That's my address, all right."

Was it something in the expression on her face, the vast difference between her education level and Zechariah's, the gap in their maturity, or perhaps the innocence in her voice that made the angel react differently this time when Mary unknowingly echoed the question that brought on Zechariah's inability to speak?

Her response to the angel began as Zechariah's response had. "How will this be?" (verse 34).

Zechariah's question had ended, "[Since] I am an old man?"

Hers ended, "Since I am a virgin?"

Zechariah was silenced for asking, for doubting.

Mary was not silenced for asking, for wondering.

Gabriel simply answered Mary with "The Holy Spirit will come on you, and the power of the Most High will overshadow you. So the holy one to be born will be called the Son of God" (verse 35).

The word *episkiazō* translated "overshadow" appears infrequently in the Bible.[1] But each time, it speaks of being enveloped and overwhelmed by the glory of God.[2]

Gabriel took time to explain to Mary—as if to comfort her and grow her young faith—that Mary's relative Elizabeth was going to give birth in her old age, "she who was said to be unable to conceive" (verse 36). He told her Elizabeth was in her sixth month.

The unable to conceive—pregnant.

The virgin—about to become pregnant . . . and in a most unusual way.

Both were miraculous. Stunning revelations.

According to Luke 1:37, the angel added one more confirmation, the stamp of *it is as good as done*, when he told Mary, "For no word from God will ever fail."

As I have, you may have read that Luke 1 passage in the past and landed your thoughts on "highly favored," or "you are to call him Jesus," or "his kingdom will never end." You may have underlined or circled "Do not be afraid." Or you may have consistently been drawn to the innocent question "How can this be?"

How can it be? How are any of the wonders we're privileged to witness possible? Because the Holy Spirit comes upon us, and the power of the Most High overshadows us. Never again will a virgin conceive as Mary did. But so much is birthed in us and so many possibilities become embryos of hope that grow to maturity when we allow the Holy Spirit to overwhelm us with the glory of God.

This key, pivotal role of the Holy Spirit in causing the conception of a holy child within a young virgin woman favored by God cannot be dismissed as a single line in an ancient story. It is a truth on which to rest our faith. And, as Gabriel said, it is proof that "no word from God will ever fail."

◆ PONDERINGS ◆

When have you needed the reassurance that God's words can't fail? Is it right now? The Advent season is bedecked with reminders for those who are looking for them.

◆ ADVENT PRAYER ◆

Open our eyes wider.
Open our hearts broader.
Open our spirits
to the work of Your Spirit
so that we don't miss the wonder
in this wonder-full season.
Amen.

The Courage to Say Yes

"Let it be to me according to your word."
Luke 1:38 ESV

*I*s your calendar filling up as Christmas draws nearer? Did you agree to commitments that have now multiplied and consumed what were once spaces?

With school programs, seasonal concerts, church special events, and two major holidays close together (for those in the United States, Thanksgiving and Christmas, with New Year celebrations just over the horizon), are you admitting to yourself this might be another online purchasing year for gifts? Are you embroiled in family discussions over how you can manage travel and other arrangements so you don't miss any of the many family gatherings, work parties, Christmas teas, and candlelight services?

Has it taken intentional effort to open this book and make these devotional thoughts part of a crowded routine in your desire to watch for the Holy Spirit's presence in the Christmas story?

The longer my Bible remains open to the first chapter of Luke, the more I'm finding I missed, and part of that relates to my own full calendar during Advent and beyond.

Mary consulted nothing before saying yes to the message God sent through Gabriel. She didn't pull out her daily planner or calendar or check dates with her parents, with whom we assume she was still living. Once she was assured the messenger was, indeed, from God, she asked no further questions.

She said yes to the most important invitation she would ever be given. She gave no consideration to any marriage plans that might have already been in the works, since she was by Jewish tradition betrothed to Joseph. Mary didn't have a twinge of regret for how her relationships with her girlfriends would change. It isn't noted that she felt sorry for herself for how strange her story would sound to gossip-hungry townspeople—or Joseph.

She said yes.

Luke 1:38 records her instant response: "I am the Lord's servant. . . . May your word to me be fulfilled." Gabriel left her presence as soon as she agreed to the plan.

Her "be it unto me according to thy word" (KJV) must have echoed in the empty room. Or did it echo throughout heaven as watching angels celebrated? "She said yes! She said yes!"

We know from other locations in Scripture that all of heaven rejoices when one of God's children makes a decision to respond with a yes to what He asks. We also know what happens when people receive an invitation to participate in what God is doing and they start listing what else they have on their calendar, what other responsibilities "must" take precedence—burying a father, "I'm too young," "I'm too old," "I can't talk so good" (see Matthew 8:21–22; Jeremiah 1:6–7; Genesis 17:17; Exodus 4:10).

Among the most contented and effective people in my circle of friends and family—perhaps yours, too—are those who listen for the voice of the Holy Spirit and live a string of consistent responses: "God asked. I said yes."

Even at her young age, and even though she wasn't yet aware of all the details or implications, Mary understood the principle. "God decreed it. The Holy Spirit will carry it out. I don't need to know more. What option would I have but to say yes?"

Revisit the holiday schedule that is building daily in your personal or family calendar. Which of the activities or opportunities do you sense were clearly God issuing the invitation? Which ones will depend on the Holy Spirit to carry out? Which activities are the work of other people's expectations for you? Which are merely societal expectations?

How would you now rank the rest in order of importance?

◆ PONDERINGS ◆

Consider these questions that might help you make your decisions about the activities that will mark this Advent season for you and your family:

1. If I say yes, will my answer be motivated by a sense of obligation to other people or by love for the Lord and obedience to His Word and will?
2. Will relationships with my family be enhanced or hampered and strained if I participate?
3. Can I miss this activity or opportunity without serious consequences or a sense of loss?
4. Am I convinced that it would build my spiritual life, or could it threaten it?

What does it take to get the heart ready for Christmas? It takes attention to our heart-focus and attitude. It takes guarding against over-commitment and fatigue that can adversely affect our approach to the holidays. It requires purposeful intention that sees through trappings and glitter, and it eliminates all but the necessary to throw the spotlight on the story that captivates as none other.

◆ ADVENT PRAYER ◆

Prepare our hearts, Lord,
to receive You,
know You,
not neglect You
in this season
of expectation.
Amen.

The Glorious Turning

"For the Mighty One has done great things for me—holy is his name."

Luke 1:49

One of the struggles we often face during Advent is not at all new—the commercialization of what Christians long to preserve as a holy season. We cringe at the coarseness, the self-centeredness, the financially outrageous, the plastic, the frosted, and the winterization of Christmas without Christ.

You're reading this because you chose to approach Advent differently—holding tight to the sacred, the God-honoring, and the Spirit-attentive remembrance of our Savior's birth.

It's not the world's intention, certainly. We've seen it recently even in the way we globally once noted "before Jesus came" and "after Jesus came" in reference to historical time-keeping. BC once meant "before Christ" and marked a clear distinction in the change in humanity who lived in the time periods before the Son of God came to earth—before He came to live among us—and after. AD once meant *Anno Domini* (Latin for "in the year of the Lord," meaning the years after Christ was born).

There's been a turning. Some have attempted to remove Christ from how we mark historical and present time as surely as public schools attempted to remove Christ from Christmas in their celebrations, songs, and breaks. It's a *holiday* break rather than a Christmas break . . . on paper. It's a *holiday* celebration without a Redeemer's birth.

You've seen the calculation of time noted now as BCE (before current era) and CE (current era).[1]

But, in an almost laughable way, they couldn't succeed in removing Christ! The abbreviations label the same time frames: before Christ and after Christ was born! The world has turned to other expressions, another acronym, but the truth of history remains that everything changed when He came.

In our search for the Holy Spirit in the Christmas story, we note clearly that the Spirit of Christmas can't be ousted by any human or spiritual force. The Spirit of Christmas is the presence that is unaffected by the world's attempts to secularize what we hold sacred.

Turning point? It remains.

Consider how the moment the Holy Spirit came upon Mary everything changed. One minute, she was a young girl anticipating a common marriage. The next minute, she was carrying within her a growing babe who would become her Lord, anticipating the world's most uncommon birth.

The Holy Spirit convicts and convinces. We're told in John, "And when He has come, He will convict the world of sin, and of righteousness, and of judgment" (16:8 NKJV). The NIV translation uses the words "prove the world to be in the wrong about" in place of the word *convict*.

The Holy Spirit turns our hearts toward Jesus. Are you thinking about Jesus this Advent? It was the Holy Spirit who drew or turned your thoughts.

> You turned the nomad shepherds
>   to a path that led them to
> a musty, dusty stable.
>   You led them straight to You.
>
> You called the myriad angels
>   from tending other things.
> You turned their hearts toward shepherd boys,
>   and toward an infant King.
>
> You turned the donkey's head
>   as he bore his burden rare.
> You turned the woman's moans to joy
>   as they split the cold night air.

You even turned the Star away
    from its accustomed route.
Its light bore right through stable roofs
    and shouted, yet stood mute.

You turned the path of wisest kings
    to journey toward the light.
You drew them with bright cords of love
    that pierced the black of night.

And now, dear Father, once again,
    the pleading is not new,
We ask that as we celebrate
    You'll turn our hearts toward You.

And we will turn our eyes upon Jesus,
    and look full in His infant face.
And the things of earth will grow strangely dim
    in the light of His glory and grace.[2]

◆ PONDERINGS ◆

Under the Holy Spirit's influence, Mary turned from peasant girl to woman-on-a-mission. What turning points can you mark in your life, before and after your encounters with Him?

◆ ADVENT PRAYER ◆

Father God, Jesus, Holy Spirit,
we are grateful
for the turning point
or points
You offered us.
As You welcomed us
to follow You,
we welcome You
to guide us through
these weeks of anticipation
and gratitude
for the Glorious Turning
that is You.
Amen.

The Morning After Mary's Moment

"I am the Lord's servant," Mary answered. "May your word to me be fulfilled."

Luke 1:38

Mary's parents are not mentioned in the Advent telling in the Bible. Were they still alive? If not, where did she live? If they were alive, did she still live with them? She had not yet moved to Joseph's house. No relatives other than Elizabeth are mentioned in Scripture.

It may be that she had still-living parents, but they had disengaged from her life. Or perhaps Mary was an orphan working as a servant in someone else's home. We won't know this side of heaven. But for the sake of pondering the kinds of things

Mary might have pondered in her heart (see Luke 2:19) after the remarkable proclamation of Gabriel and the unprecedented encounter with the Holy Spirit, let's let imagination paint a picture for us.

How might she have handled informing her parents?

• • •

Part 1

Mary heard her mother rustling about in the kitchen. It was early, but it wasn't uncommon for her mother to be already tackling the tasks of cooking and cleaning, readying the house for her family. It was unusual, however, for Mary to be lying in bed, listening.

It's not that Mary was half-asleep. She hadn't slept at all. Early morning grogginess hadn't kept her in bed. It was her late-night visitor and his startling message . . . and her current reluctance to share that message with her family.

What she'd heard in the night—and what happened to her— would change everything.

In the pale light of dawn, she stopped the wild musings of her mind, slid from the protection of her bedcovers, and quickly dressed for the day. As she pulled her homespun sheath over her head, her hands rested briefly on her abdomen . . . on the spot where the child was already growing undetectably. Small and oddly helpless. Imagine. God's Son. Tiny and vulnerable and helpless, depending on her!

"Well, good morning, Mary! I wondered if I'd have to tip your bed on end to get you rousted this day. Oh, I must show you what I did in the night!"

"In the night?"

"Yes, for some reason, I was stirred awake. There I was in the middle of the night, wide awake but content and at peace. No nightmare shook me. It was as if I'd felt a breeze blow through the house. Strange, isn't it?"

"Yes, Ima. Very strange."

"After a time, the sense grew even stronger, as if I were being called to a mission of some kind. After lying there staring at the ceiling for a time, I rose and came out here, stoked the fire, and sat before it praying."

"Praying?"

"I prayed until the burden lifted some hours later, then got up with what I believe is a brilliant plan for your wedding meal. Look at what I've sketched out here. I hope you'll be pleased. Your father sold that tapestry he was hanging on to."

"What?"

"He always insisted it would be worth something someday. He sold it to one of the vendors in the marketplace yesterday. Traded it for the promise of a fine beef animal. We'll have succulent beef for the wedding feast, rather than our poor chickens and mutton only! Won't that be a treat? Mary, what's wrong? Are you ill?"

"Mother, I'm . . . I'm pregnant."

"What? You're not . . . I need to sit. We've never allowed you and Joseph to be alone for even a short time. There's always a family member with you."

"It wasn't Joseph, Mother."

"What are you saying? This will crush him . . . and your father! How far along are you?"

"A few hours."

"A few *hours*? You're not making any sense. Oh, your beautiful wedding garment! And the plans we've made. How will we keep the town elders from finding out? The rules are strict right now, Mary. Your betrothal to Joseph may mean that they'll consider this an act of adultery!"

"I realize."

"Child, I can't lose you over a foolish mistake. We'll find you a place to hide. Perhaps with your cousin Elizabeth. I shudder to think of it—the baby is my own *grandchild*, after all—but have you considered allowing Elizabeth to raise the child as her own? Her barrenness is a crushing burden for her, and you are so young, and not experienced in the ways of the world. Or"—Ima paused—"perhaps you have had far more experience than I ever dreamed."

"Mother!"

"Who is he? Who is the villain who took advantage of my precious daughter?"

"No one took advantage of me, Ima. I . . . cooperated. An angel visited me in the night. And he told me that I am to bear the Christ child, the Son of God."

"You? Did this angel happen to mention why you?"

"He said I was being shown favor from on high."

"You're little more than a child yourself. Why you?"

"I don't know, Ima."

"All our nation's talk about the coming Messiah—it's filled your head full of fantasies until you've dreamed up this notion that of all people God Almighty would choose you, a peasant girl. And now you think you're pregnant!"

"I believe I am, Mother. Already I feel different inside."

"Well of course you do, silly girl. You're concocting a lie."

"But I'm not."

"What was this angel wearing . . . and keep in mind when you answer that I know a good bit of religious history."

"All I saw was light. But I heard his voice. I don't know how else to explain it to you. For reasons I can't even begin to imagine, God has chosen me to bear His Son. The Holy Spirit came upon me in the night and—"

"Now, this is ludicrous!"

". . . and in a few months, I will give birth to a son, and I'll call His name Jesus."

"Jesus?"

"God asked this of me. How could I say no?"

"Simple. 'No.' Or, 'Could you give me a minute to think about this, Michael?'"

"It wasn't Michael."

"What?"

"It wasn't the angel Michael. It was Gabriel."

"Oh, you two had a nice little conversation, did you? The angel Gabriel walked into your room last night and said to a girl who barely knows how to make a decent loaf of bread, 'Are you busy for the next nine months? Want to have a baby? Want to have God's baby?'"

"Mother, I beg you to listen to me. Have I ever lied to you before?"

"No. I think that almost makes it harder on me now, Mary. What's happened to you?"

"Is it so unusual for God to choose someone unworthy but willing? Is that not the pattern He's used from the beginning of time? Moses . . . Joshua . . . Gideon . . ."

"But, it can't be."

"Why not?"

"Because . . . because of what this will cost you if it is true. Oh, child!"

◆ PONDERINGS ◆

We can identify with even an imagined scene of what Mary's acceptance of God's plan and the Holy Spirit's visit would mean for Mary. The Spirit of God often calls us to tasks and assignments the world around us doesn't understand. Caring for a difficult aging parent. Forgiving the undeserving. Leaving a sense of security to dare bravely for God. How do we explain it to those who don't understand?

By leaning on the Spirit who called us.

◆ ADVENT PRAYER ◆

Spirit of God,
thank You for not leaving Mary
or us
alone
as we carry out
the assignments and adventures
into which You have
invited us.
Soften our hearts
to be eager
with our yes
to You.
Amen.

The Aftermath of a Miracle

Then Mary responded, saying, "Yes! I will be a mother for the Lord! As his servant, I accept whatever he has for me. May everything you have told me come to pass."

Luke 1:38 TPT

Our imaginations are hard at work all day every day. No matter our job, our family situation, or the maturity of our faith, we're constantly using the gift of imagination to dream, plan, consider, and wonder. It can get us into trouble if our imagination focuses on fears or worries or if it leads us astray of biblical truth.

The story we started yesterday in our Advent devotions was a work of imagination that filled in gaps of what the Bible doesn't specify. But whether true to what actually happened or not, it fits with what we know about Mary, what we know about mothers of pregnant teens, and what we know about our own insecurities and how we react when presented with a God-shaped task for a human-shaped vessel with human reactions and limited insight.

It also fits with what we're discovering about the role and the compassion of the Holy Spirit in this story of all stories that we celebrate during Advent. Where might God-formed imagination take us in Part 2 the morning after the Holy Spirit's presence in Mary's room and heart?

•••

Part 2

Mary reached tentatively to embrace her mother.

"Is it possible, Ima, that what stirred you awake in the night was the Holy Spirit calling you to pray for me while I faced the decision to accept or reject what Gabriel was suggesting? Already this morning, I've begun to bear the consequences of saying yes."

"Oh, daughter!"

"The angel didn't ask me. He told me what God said would happen. My choice was only in the attitude I would take . . . receiving his message and these consequences as a gift, as a call on my life, or straining and fighting against them. Do you think it would be healthy for the baby if I closed my heart and grew bitter? Have we not both seen the unhappy children of bitter women?"

"But Mary . . ."

"I know I am very young and that I am far from being ready or prepared for this assignment. But please don't shut me out. Before this is over, I believe I will be asked to bear far more than just the weight of a child."

● ▶ ▲

No one but God knows the true reaction of Mary's family (if she still had one) when she shared that she had been chosen to be the birth mother of His Son. Any story written about it, including the previous vignette, is a fabrication of human imagination based on the kind of reactions a loving, caring, but startled family might have if the story was happening today.

What we are told is that as soon as Mary agreed to what God decreed, the angel departed (see Luke 1:38). He did not stay to walk her through all the details, holding her hand and coaching her about how to break the news to her parents or how to cope with gossipy neighbors and vengeful town elders.

The angel, the messenger, didn't stay. But the Holy Spirit did. The One who "came upon her" and "overshadowed" her, whose power bypassed the traditional methods for a woman to become pregnant, also emboldened her, sustained her, and guided her through the repercussions of her willingness to accept the Word—and the child—of promise.

The Holy Spirit's role was not finished after Jesus was miraculously conceived. He was there with His comforting shoulder for Mary to lean on.

In our own lives, too, the messenger may not remain. But the Holy Spirit does.

◆ PONDERINGS ◆

In your search for the Holy Spirit's presence embedded in the Advent story, what elements have brought you comfort? Is it something different for other members of your family?

◆ ADVENT PRAYER ◆

Thank You, Holy Spirit,
for the role You played
in comforting
young Mary
so that even Jesus's earthly family
and we
would know Your peace.
Amen.

Wait Until I Tell Elizabeth!

Afterward, Mary arose and hurried off to the hill country of
Judea, to the village where Zechariah and Elizabeth lived.

Luke 1:39 TPT

*W*hat happened next after Mary's encounter with
Gabriel and with the Holy Spirit's "coming upon"
her is recorded in Luke 1:39, one verse after Mary
said yes and the angel departed. We're told Mary packed and
hurried to the town in the hill country where Elizabeth and
Zechariah lived.

Sounds like a "Do not pass Go; do not collect two hundred
dollars" moment from a Monopoly game. Nothing else is recorded between what we now call the immaculate conception
and Mary running for the hills.

She likely traveled on foot, as most did in those days. We're told it was a journey of almost one hundred miles and would have taken four days to a week. Close to marathon distance every day. Mary was determined, undeterred, and courageous. Whether she joined other travelers well-known to her or remained solo—which had to have been a daunting proposition—we're not given insight to that information.

Did she follow a well-worn path? How did she respond when people asked where she was headed? Who but the Holy Spirit could have protected a young girl on a journey like that? Have you considered the presence of the Holy Spirit divinely watching over and defending Mary in the briefly mentioned but arduous trip to Elizabeth's house?

We also have no record that she informed Joseph before she left. Unlike today's engaged couples, they wouldn't have texted multiple times a day. According to Jewish custom, the betrothal period could last as long as a year. The bride-to-be and her groom might not see each other often during that time. How long might it have been before Joseph even realized she was gone?

Nothing in the biblical record tells us more than Mary packed and headed out. She may have simply disappeared from her normal responsibilities and community connections. If she told anyone, would it have been a surprise that she decided to visit her relative Elizabeth?

Through the angel Gabriel, the Holy Spirit used Elizabeth's condition as confirmation that the word Mary heard was true. He said, "What's more, Elizabeth is having a baby!" (see Luke 1:36, author's paraphrase). If anyone could understand the upheaval of emotions Mary was experiencing, it would be Elizabeth.

What forms might the Holy Spirit have taken during that journey? Did His voice whisper encouragement to Mary when she grew tired? Did He appear as a protector when ne'er-do-wells threatened the girl? Did He walk beside her in some visible form? Did He recite ancient texts that affirmed what was happening within her?

One thing about a journey of many days is that it affords a lot of elbow room for thoughts to wander. Where were Mary's? Maybe what she needed protection from was not threatening thieves but her own internal dialogue.

What was she thinking on mile forty—too far to abandon the journey, not close enough to see her destination? Would she have had no doubts, no questions, no imagined conversations about how she'd greet Elizabeth, if they would even receive her once they heard her news, or how she would tell Joseph when the time came?

"First, he'll say . . . Then I'll say . . . And then he'll divorce me. What honorable man would believe the story I have to tell?"

Or was every step of her travel marked by prayer, a continual recitation of what she knew of the Torah, what she'd overheard in conversations, a rehearsal of the night the angel and the Spirit came to her? Or was every footstep punctuated with a single phrase—"Be. It. Done. To. Me. According. To. Your. Word."

Even said slowly, she would have had time to repeat her commitment almost twenty-two thousand times, with the occasional break for a fig cake or a bite of bread and an opportunity to fill her water vessel from a roadside well.

Even at her young age, Mary would have known that not all early pregnancies reach full term. Did she concern herself with the strain on her body and the child forming inside? Or did the Holy Spirit cradle the child, too?

Too many questions? Or do we ask too few?

We accept the truth of what happened. Mary journeyed one hundred miles to Elizabeth and Zechariah's home. Maybe we miss evidence of the Holy Spirit's presence if we don't ask questions about the details.

Our faith, of which the birth of Christ is one of several hinge points, is not opinion-based or anyone spouting, "The way I see it . . ." But it is a pondering faith.

Later in the story of Christ's birth, after the shepherds spread the news about the wonders surrounding Jesus's entrance into the world, Mary "kept all these things, and pondered them in her heart" (Luke 2:19 KJV).

I have a feeling that's what she was doing all nine months, including on the long walk to hear about Elizabeth's miracle and to help her relative with her own questions.

The Spirit often moves people to get up and go. As we'll see in the scene when Mary arrives at her destination, Mary had been compelled by the Holy Spirit to take the trip. Without it, so much would be missing that now puts us in awe.

◆ PONDERINGS ◆

Mary "pondered these things in her heart," as we just read. What have you been pondering deep within either this past year, or during past weeks, or in this Advent season in anticipation of celebrating Christ's birth? What thoughts have lingered? Are they God-honoring thoughts? If not, now is the moment to evict them so that you are not distracted from what the Holy Spirit may be whispering to you in your journey.

◆ ADVENT PRAYER ◆

Holy Spirit,
clear my mind
of anything that
diverts my attention
away from what You
want to teach me,
show me,
change in me.
Amen.

An Unborn Child Dances in the Spirit

> When Elizabeth heard Mary's greeting, the baby leaped in her womb.
>
> Luke 1:41

Whatever way Mary might have imagined how she would've been received at Elizabeth and Zechariah's house, could she have anticipated what unfolded? When Mary entered their home and called out a greeting to Elizabeth—which makes us assume Elizabeth was in a different part of the house or Mary was in the courtyard only and Elizabeth within the structure—all heaven broke loose.

"When Elizabeth heard Mary's greeting, the baby leaped in her womb, and Elizabeth was filled with the Holy Spirit" (Luke

1:41). Most Bible translations spell it out that clearly. The baby *leaped* in her womb.

For a woman who is by this time six months pregnant, would that be unusual? How did Elizabeth know this was no ordinary baby flutter, no standard version of an unborn child's arm or leg exercises? Was it perhaps the first time she'd *felt* the movement that had likely been happening for two months or more? Was it confirmation of the Holy Spirit's promise to her and Zechariah that the baby would indeed *be born healthy* despite Elizabeth's advanced age and all the complications that might bring? Was it reassurance for her?

Or are we allowing too much time for the "and" in that sentence of Scripture?

The baby leaped *and* Elizabeth was filled with the Holy Spirit. A baby dancing in the Spirit inside would make any woman break out her own moves.

The Spirit's presence within her opened her mouth wide—the woman whose husband was at this time still mute. In a loud voice, by the way, Elizabeth declared to Mary, "Blessed are you among women, and blessed is the child you will bear!" (Luke 1:42).

The Passion Translation uses the phrase "she prophesied with power."

The Spirit imparted knowledge to her that Elizabeth could not have known. Unmarried Mary was also expecting, by this time only by a week or a little more. The Word of God doesn't tell us that Mary spilled her story first. The wonder is that Elizabeth just knew. By what means? The Holy Spirit.

Elizabeth, the wife of a Jewish priest, became a pregnant prophetess in that moment. "But why am I so favored, that the mother of my Lord should come to me?" (verse 43).

Elizabeth and Mary shared the same questions about why they would have been favored by God. When Elizabeth first saw Mary and asked Mary her question, that might have been the first time Mary heard herself called a mother. But beyond that, Elizabeth's exclamation revealed that the Holy Spirit had informed her about what only Mary and the Holy Spirit knew at the time. The child inside Mary, microscopic then, was Elizabeth's Lord.

"As soon as the sound of your greeting reached my ears," she said, "the baby in my womb leaped for joy. Blessed is she who has believed that the Lord would fulfill his promises to her!" (verses 44–45).

Who is the *she* in that sentence? *Who* believed that the Lord would fulfill His promises to her? Both of the women. They'd been promised impossible things. They both believed the angel's message and accepted God's assignment for them. Elizabeth's baby's response to being in the presence of his Lord and King Jesus—dancing in the Spirit while only weighing four or five pounds and without sight to aid him or understanding of anything other than "This is God at work!"—strengthened the solidity of their faith.

And ours.

We, today, believe that John was John and Jesus was Jesus, that Elizabeth and Mary were chosen for radically important roles, that the child in Mary was there by the power of the Holy Spirit, because a *fetus* recognized *a week-old pregnancy* as divine. Because an unborn child recognized a work of the Holy Spirit when it drew near.

Oh, my.

Sometimes we casually rattle off Psalm 139:15–16 (emphasis added):

> My frame was not hidden from you
> > when I was made in the secret place,
> > when I was woven together in the depths of the
> > earth.
> **Your eyes saw my unformed body;**
> > all the days ordained for me were written in your
> > book
> before one of them came to be.

Or we take too little note of Jeremiah 1:5 (emphasis added) when God through the Holy Spirit appears to Jeremiah in a dream and says:

> "Before **I formed you** in the womb I knew you,
> **before you were born I set you apart;**
> I appointed you as a prophet to the nations."

Mary was the first to know that the child in her womb was conceived by the Holy Spirit. Elizabeth was the second, from what we gather in biblically recorded history. The unborn John, later known as John the Baptizer, was the third. Imagine.

Both babes were already devoted to God and His plan for them, long before their minds registered conscious thought.

If that baby's leap for joy doesn't inspire awe in us, it certainly did for Mary. What follows Elizabeth's body-rattling baby leap is the soul-stirring, poetic-turned-prophetic song many recognize as "The Magnificat."

It begins, "My soul glorifies the Lord and my spirit rejoices in God my Savior." You can read Mary's full faith-filled song in Luke 1:46–55.

Her spirit rejoiced in what *His* Spirit had done and was doing.

◆ PONDERINGS ◆

Are both Elizabeth's and Mary's responses your response? As you and your family journey through this Advent season, will your spirit celebrate what the Holy Spirit did long ago? And what the Holy Spirit is doing in your life and faith walk today?

◆ ADVENT PRAYER ◆

Whatever might keep my feet
firmly rooted
to the floor of responsibilities
and expectations,
may it not prevent me
from dancing with joy
over my coming King!
Amen.

Mary as a Long-Term Houseguest

Mary stayed with Elizabeth for about three months and then returned home.

Luke 1:56

After the almost week-long trek to Elizabeth and Zechariah's home, we might assume Mary would stay with them for a few days to recover from her journey before returning home, just as holiday guests who travel from a distance and force us to turn the depository for all the stuff-we-haven't-dealt-with back into a guest room.

Mary stayed for three months.

For most pregnant women, the first trimester and the last trimester are the most challenging. Those two bookend three-month periods are often marked by extreme fatigue as the body first adjusts to the presence of a growing baby and adjusts radically again in preparation for birth.

Mary and Elizabeth were both in the bookend trimesters—first and last—while they spent those three months together before Mary returned home. Remember the Bible's reference to Elizabeth's *inability* to conceive? That means the experience was a first for both women.

It's also noteworthy that Elizabeth had sequestered herself at home for the first five months. So, the companionship Mary and Elizabeth shared during Mary's extended stay feels especially significant.

Elizabeth's godly and faithful husband, Zechariah, hadn't spoken a word to her for half a year. They'd shared no verbal conversations the entire time Elizabeth was pregnant. Oh, the mom-to-be might have been speaking, and the dad-to-be may have tried to respond, but Elizabeth was unable to hear her husband's voice. They'd lost their ability to banter and discuss a topic through to a conclusion because Zechariah had doubted God could pull off giving them a child and was rendered mute.

But with Mary living in their home, Elizabeth's long-withheld words had a place to land and engage another person who cared about her.

What would they have talked about for three months?

Babies.

No doubt.

"Elizabeth, show me how to create nappies out of scraps of fabric."

"Mary, I've never made a diaper. Let's check YouTube."

"How long is a baby supposed to sleep?"

"I'm an old woman! I hope they nap as much as I need to."

We can envision conversations something like that. But isn't it plausible many of their discussions revolved around what they had in common spiritually? They'd both had remarkable encounters with the Holy Spirit.

As had Zechariah.

The three of them—Zechariah, Mary, and Elizabeth—were, according to biblical records, the first three people to "hear" from God after four hundred years of silence because of their nation's rebellion against Him.

Three mere humans. An old man, an old woman, and a young girl. The soon coming of the Messiah broke through the sound barrier. How could the Holy Spirit's presence among them and words to them not have been the hot topic of most of their dinner-table talks?

Poor Zechariah. His hands or writing implement must have been flying trying to keep up with all he'd experienced and was learning while the women chatted freely.

As we've crossed over into December and into the holiday season, is the Holy Spirit a hot topic around your dinner table? If He is, that would perfectly fit with what might have been happening in those three months when Mary occupied the guest room in the home of her relatives.

Advent is about anticipation. The most common synonyms, according to Merriam-Webster, are *arrival, appearance, dawn, entrance, emergence, debut, birth*. Our Advent season is anticipation of Jesus's debut on earth's scene. Although long predicted, the first whispers that "the time had come" were delivered to three people who huddled together in a house in the hill country of Judea.

One was speechless. One was nearing the birth of a child she'd stopped dreaming she might ever have. The other was holding her breath through the first trimester, astounded that of all the women in the world, she'd been chosen to bear God's Son.

An unlikely trio, to say the least. But they were joined by singularly spectacular and life-altering encounters with the Holy Spirit.

Did you know that although he may have made unnamed appearances elsewhere, Gabriel—who delivered messages from God to the three—is named only three times in Scripture? Gabriel appeared to Daniel in the Old Testament (see Daniel 8:16; 9:21, 23—also considered "highly esteemed"), to Zechariah with a message for Zechariah and Elizabeth (see Luke 1:19), and to Mary, the mother of Jesus (see Luke 1:26).

Our unlikely trio had been called to challenging roles (as had Daniel). No wonder they needed months to strengthen one another in the Spirit.

◆ PONDERINGS ◆

Who in your circle of family and friends needs the freedom to talk with you, to be strengthened in the Spirit or undergirded in their faith, as Christmas draws nearer? An unexpectedly pregnant woman? A new widow or widower? Someone with an unnerving diagnosis? A church friend estranged from family? A lonely person with a too-long empty guest room?

◆ ADVENT PRAYER ◆

*May my ears
be attuned to
the needs of others
for whom this season
has thrown a spotlight
on their life circumstances.
Holy Spirit,
send Your comfort
through me.
Amen.*

Baby Names

> To everyone's surprise he wrote, "His name is John."
>
> Luke 1:63 NLT

Baby names were not a topic of conversation between Elizabeth and Mary. In all of history, they may have been two of a very small club of women who didn't concern themselves with the choice of their baby's name.

It wasn't discussed because the names had already been decided and handed to them by Gabriel, the Lord's messenger. The boys' names were John and Jesus. Done.

The community members and other relatives hadn't gotten the memo. They assumed Elizabeth's newborn, who arrived shortly after (we assume) Mary returned to her own home, would be named Zechariah, Jr., after his father. It was tradition at the time, but especially since Zechariah was still locked in the dire state of muteness, poor guy.

When Elizabeth insisted the infant boy was to be named John, the townspeople tried to talk her out of it. "None of your relatives have a name like John. You really should have considered having the epidural." (For their real words, see Luke 1:61.)

Then, in what must have seemed like a comedy act to Elizabeth and other thinkers, the villagers made hand signals to Zechariah to find out his opinion. He wasn't deaf. He was mute. The Bible doesn't tell us he lost his hearing. He lost his ability to *speak*. But there they were, using their version of sign language to find out what Daddy wanted to name his son.

In a gesture that must have been very familiar after almost a year of not speaking, Zechariah motioned for a writing tablet. He wrote four short, crisp words: "His name is John."

Tradition flew out the window. Expectations did not win out over God's will.

Before Zechariah even laid aside the tablet, his voice returned! The restoration of his ability to speak silenced the crowd. And we're told his first words were worship, praise to God (see verse 64). During the nine months of Elizabeth's pregnancy, something new had been forming in Zechariah, too. Unshakable faith.

Like Mary, his praise was birthed in the form of poetry or a song. Verse 67 of Luke 1 says that at that very moment, Zechariah was "filled with the Holy Spirit." It's startling to realize how much of the Christmas story relates that key players were or would be "filled with the Holy Spirit."

"Praise be to the Lord, the God of Israel," Zechariah said under the *influence* of the Holy Spirit, "because he has come to his people and redeemed them" (Luke 1:68).

Redeemed. Past tense. In Zechariah's eyes, even though the birth of Jesus was still about six months in the future, the arrival of the Messiah was as good as done. He prophesied what was to come.

Within that prophesy is a sweet message from Zechariah's lips to the eight-day-old son he held in his arms. "And you, my child, will be called a prophet of the Most High; for you will go on before the Lord to prepare the way for him" (Luke 1:76).

So much must have been pent up within Zechariah after his long silence. Doubt had closed his mouth. His no-matter-what obedience to God's plan opened it.

We learned earlier that Scripture tells us Mary stayed with Elizabeth and Zechariah for "about" three months before returning to Nazareth. Have you ever wondered if Mary remained at Elizabeth's side until John was born, helping Elizabeth through the birthing process? We can't read between the lines and form our theology or convictions on that. But we can wonder about what isn't specified.

In some ways, because of the relationship they must have developed, it would seem strange if Mary had abandoned Elizabeth shortly before the birth. Mary may well have been there to witness it—and learn. She may have attended the birth not as an expert but as a comfort.

Wouldn't you imagine—with Elizabeth's unborn child's profound reaction to the babe within Mary—Elizabeth would have longed to have the Redeemer close? Hope grew within Mary, and Elizabeth knew it. Mary may have washed the vernix, the creamy white layer of protection, from the baby's birth-reddened head and body. Imagine if Mary had actually cradled John the Baptist's head moments after his birth!

Would she have stayed for the naming ceremony? Elizabeth and Zechariah's story was part of her own. Would Mary have heard Zechariah proclaim with now unfettered lips, "His name is John!"? And might that moment have infused courage into young Mary? *It is happening as the Holy Spirit said.*

Whether Mary stayed for the birth and naming eight days later or returned home earlier at the urging of responsibilities or the move of the Spirit, how full her heart must have been on the long journey home. It had been fourteen generations of people since anyone had reported seeing or hearing from God. Not fourteen years. Fourteen generations! She had witnessed that silence broken in her time, in her own body.

When Gabriel appeared to Zechariah to give him a promise from God and a baby name, the current-day unfolding of their ancient faith was kindled. A Savior was coming. Zechariah's son would be the forerunner. And Mary's son would be the long-awaited God-in-the-flesh Messiah.

In our Bibles, there is one thing—a title page only—between the last words of the book of Malachi and the beginning of the New Testament heralding the arrival of Jesus. Malachi concludes with God prophesying that He would send a forerunner like Elijah who would "turn the hearts of the parents to their children, and the hearts of the children to their parents" (Malachi 4:6).

If that sounds familiar, it may be because we read it in the story of Gabriel's additional words to Zechariah. After the four-hundred-year gap, Gabriel brought God's message, which included Luke 1:17: "And he will go on before the Lord, in the spirit and power of Elijah, to turn the hearts of the parents to their children and the disobedient to the wisdom of the righteous—to make ready a people prepared for the Lord."

We've been reading about an Advent approach to prepare our hearts for the Christmas season so we don't miss the significance of Christ's birth and the Spirit/spirit of Christmas. Observing the connecting pieces is part of our personal Advent journey. Gabriel, Zechariah, Elizabeth, Mary, John, Jesus, impossible babies, specific names, and the Spirit filling those who were receptive to the holy and remarkable.

◆ PONDERINGS ◆

What was in Zechariah's song? Read Luke 1:76–79, and linger on the power words. Zechariah prophesied that Jesus would give His people "the **knowledge** of **salvation** through the **forgiveness** of their sins" and that Jesus would "**shine** on those living in darkness and in the shadow of death, to **guide** our feet into the path of **peace**."

◆ ADVENT PRAYER ◆

*May our thoughts linger
not on what is left to do
as Christmas approaches
but on what
the Spirit spoke,
the Word prophesied,
and on what You, Jesus,
have already done for us.
Amen.*

How Did Joseph Find Out?

"Take Mary home as your wife, because what is conceived
in her is from the Holy Spirit."

Matthew 1:20

H ow much time do you suppose Mary spent fretting
over how she would inform Joseph, her betrothed,
about the angel visit and Gabriel's proclamation? It
would have been worry misspent.

Joseph already knew . . . or did he?

As often as I've heard the story, I've assumed Mary would
have told Joseph right away. But a tiny detail in the Word says
that Mary "with haste" packed and took off for Elizabeth's place.

I've even pondered, as you may have, that Mary needed the
three months with Elizabeth to figure out how she was going
to break the news to Joseph.

Even as young as she was, Mary would have known the law that if Mary was pregnant, Joseph would have every legal right to "divorce" her from the binding decree that considered them "married" on paper before their actual wedding. It's a Jewish tradition thing.

And claiming that she'd not been with a man would have been considered the lamest excuse in the book, since an immaculate conception had never happened in the history of the world. History . . . of . . . the . . . world!

Never mind that Mary knew it was miraculous. Joseph hadn't been there. *He* hadn't heard the angel speak to her or sensed the presence of the Holy Spirit overshadowing her.

But the Holy Spirit misses no detail.

I've often encouraged an unnecessarily concerned friend, "God doesn't do half-miracles." No member of the Trinity—Father, Son, or Holy Spirit—ever does anything halfway or fails to consider the consequences of what is revealed, instructed, asked, or required.

An angel was dispatched to Joseph, Mary's husband on paper or husband-to-be waiting for the ceremony. The angel's purpose? To assure the man that what was happening with Mary wasn't a ruse, a moral failure on her part, or a disruption in God's plan for them as a couple.

Luke's record of the Christmas story doesn't include that detail, but the book of Matthew does, perhaps because it was through Joseph's family tree that the Messiah was predicted to come.

"This is how the birth of Jesus the Messiah came about: His mother Mary was pledged to be married to Joseph, but before they came together, she was found to be pregnant through the Holy Spirit" (Matthew 1:18).

Can you see the headlines in the *Nazareth News? Woman Found Pregnant Through the Holy Spirit.*

Not quite how it happened. But word did get around, even before the advent (see what I did there?) of newspapers and social media.

The Matthew account tells us, "Because Joseph her husband was faithful to the law, and yet did not want to expose her to public disgrace, he had in mind to divorce her quietly" (Matthew 1:19).

Let's push pause. What might have happened to Mary if Joseph had broken their marriage agreement? Even if done as kindly as possible? Mary could have been a single mom her entire life. But there's more, and it is a display of the Holy Spirit's attention to detail.

The Messiah had long been expected to be born in the lineage—from the family tree—of King David. If Joseph had divorced Mary, Jesus would not have fulfilled that prophecy.

What to do, what to do?

An angel of the Lord (unnamed) appeared to Joseph in a dream and said, "Joseph son of David" (verse 20).

There we go. *Let's make it clear*, the angel noted, *that you have a father, and a grandfather, and several great-grandfathers,*

Joseph, but if you trace back far enough, you belong to the line of King David.

Despite—or rather because of—Joseph's mental wrestling match over his next move after hearing Mary was pregnant, the angel told Joseph not to be afraid, to "take Mary home as your wife, because what is conceived in her is from the Holy Spirit. She will give birth to a son, and you are to give him the name Jesus, because he will save his people from their sins" (Matthew 1:20–21).

We've asked the question "Where is the Holy Spirit in the Christmas story, and how does that affect our Advent preparations, our spiritual readiness to read about, discuss, and celebrate the birth of Jesus?"

He's everywhere!

Joseph wasn't just told, "Don't worry about Mary and her 'news,' Joseph. It'll be okay." Instead, he was told clearly that she wasn't lying when she said the child was conceived by the Holy Spirit.

Joseph invited her into the embrace of his home and invited the child she carried into the royal heritage of his family line. That is no small thing. Matthew 1:22 tells us, "All this took place to fulfill what the Lord had said" way back in the book of Isaiah.

What changed Joseph's mind? What moved him from considering walking away from the drama? Two words: Holy Spirit.

Confirmed. This is a work of the Holy Spirit, even if you don't understand it, Joseph.

At the words *Holy Spirit*, his heart was at peace.

Imagine if we were as easily convinced. *If the Holy Spirit is in it, I can bear anything, endure anything, and adjust my life to fit around His words. I can rest in the confidence that the Holy Spirit is with me and within me, so no assignment, no challenge, no crisis can rattle me.*

Joseph was intentionally signing up for marriage to a woman with a wild story to tell and the pending arrival of another mouth to feed. And not only a child, but a holy child. What would that cost him?

It didn't matter. Once he knew it was all part of God's plan and a work of the Holy Spirit, he set aside his concerns and obeyed what he'd been told to do.

Remember that little line—"Joseph . . . was faithful to the law" (verse 19)? Doesn't that make his reaction all the more remarkable? The laws of society dictated one thing. The voice of the Lord enabled a different response. And the Spirit empowered Joseph to follow through with what was asked of him.

◆ PONDERINGS ◆

What hard thing is being asked of you this season? Is a difficult relationship making holiday get-together plans awkward? Is illness interrupting everything? Is your calendar filled with fine print to cram it all in? Has a recent loss put a damper on the joy aspect of Advent?

The Spirit of God is as present for you as for Joseph or any other person in the Christmas story who faced something hard. Feel free to lean on Him to get you through.

◆ ADVENT PRAYER ◆

*For every hard thing
in front of us
or behind us this season,
we pray You will
empower us to
lean on You,
trust You,
and find our peace
in You alone.
Amen.*

Day 17

Mary's Nesting Months

. . . and then returned home.

Luke 1:56

The traditional candles many Christians light during Advent represent four distinct layers of anticipation as Christmas Day approaches. They symbolize a growing illumination—more candles shining—as the four weeks of Advent progress from the Sunday closest to November 30 to Christmas Day. The tradition culminates with the lighting of a center white candle that symbolizes that the Light of the world—Jesus—has come.

Beginning with the fourth Sunday before Christmas, the first candle represents hope and is sometimes called the Prophet's candle. The second week's candle represents peace and is sometimes called the Bethlehem candle. The third symbolizes joy and is sometimes known as the Shepherd's candle. And the fourth represents love.[1]

Some Advent traditions trace back to as long ago as the fourth or fifth century. The hope, peace, joy, and love that inspired the traditions trace back much further than that.

In our intentionality about searching for and celebrating the presence of the Holy Spirit during the four weeks of Advent, we've seen all four represented. Hope fulfilled. Peace realized. Joy so great it caused an unborn child to dance. Love poured out and expressed in countless ways.

The peace candle, also known as the Bethlehem candle, intrigues me. We've seen Joseph's concern and mental upheaval about the woman he'd intended to marry change to deep peace.

The circumstances hadn't changed. Life hadn't suddenly gotten easier. In fact, it had grown decidedly harder with Mary's unique pregnancy and Joseph's anticipation of the addition of the role of parent to his responsibilities. Consider the dramatic shift in his schedule upon bringing Mary into his home and the no-doubt wagging tongues of community members who had *not* been visited by the Holy Spirit.

Mary was brought to his home. But whether by divine decree or Joseph's sense of propriety and honor, Joseph pledged not to lie with her until weeks or months after Jesus was born (see Matthew 1:25). Mary remained a virgin until after Jesus arrived.

Peace came because life got less complicated? No. That's the wonder of the peace the Holy Spirit brings us. Complications don't shake that brand of peace.

For the next couple of months, the two must have been smothered by details. Mary adjusting to Joseph's home and temperament, setting up a household with her touch in it, making or collecting baby garments and other necessities. Joseph adjusting to having a woman in the house who craved sweet treats and barbeque-flavored potato chips. Both of them embroiled in long conversations about what this holy arrival would mean for their little family. They weren't given all the details of what it would be like to parent their Savior. Who wouldn't wonder what lay ahead?

Mary and Joseph were people of strong faith, chosen by God. They likely knew many of the prophecies about the coming Messiah. So, it's not hard to imagine a conversation like this:

"Joseph, we have to move to Bethlehem. The prophet said the child would be born in Bethlehem."

"We're not moving."

"But Joseph—"

"Not yet. The Spirit will tell us when the time is right. Or the government will."

Imagine. The tax collectors and census takers, the least likely to listen to God, played a vital role in the story, responding to the Spirit as they unknowingly brought all in alignment with what had been prophesied hundreds of years earlier. A census was ordered for the purpose of keeping track of the people and their tax responsibilities. And that fit perfectly with God's long-predicted plan.

He can use anything, even those who do not bow to Him.

When the decree went out from the Roman emperor that "all the world should be taxed" (Luke 2:1 KJV), Joseph and young Mary were included. Bethlehem (City of David) was the town of Joseph's lineage. An equivalent for us might be our needing to travel to the county seat to be registered—back in the days before online registration was a thing.

Would Joseph and Mary have embarked on a long journey with the child due so soon? The trip that would take them almost straight south of Nazareth was—get this—ninety miles, four or five days or more on foot, traveling eight hours per day. Except for the lack of dramatic elevation changes, that would have been almost a duplication of Mary's journey to the home of Zechariah and Elizabeth.

And if Mary's pregnancy was at all normal, it's likely she was already experiencing what we now call Braxton-Hicks contractions, and her ankles would've been the size of camel ankles. Is that where the word *cankles* comes from?

Knowing what we do about both Mary and Joseph and their openness to whatever God asked of them, we can well imagine that they embarked on their journey hemmed in peace.

Census, ugh. Taxes, double-ugh. Traveling this late in the pregnancy? Risky, perhaps even dangerous, and undoubtedly difficult for both of them—the uncomfortable mother and her concerned husband.

Except for the peace the Spirit slathered all over the situation.

Ancient texts of Scripture informed them that Bethlehem, David's hometown, would be the scene of the momentous event. They might not have known the day or the hour, but the parents knew the prophet's foretelling. And they'd witnessed what the Holy Spirit could do with a surrendered heart.

The peace they'd experienced over the months since the Holy Spirit's engagement with both mom-to-be and dad-to-be did not abandon them when they received the Roman government's directive that they were to travel to Bethlehem. Rather, it likely bolstered them with yet another confirmation that God was in this, working His plan, that they could trust Him, and that the Spirit would not wait for them back in Nazareth.

He would accompany them every step of the journey.

◆ PONDERINGS ◆

If you're human, it's likely something has challenged you in recent months. It may have grown more complicated as the year has drawn to an end. This Advent preparation time is drawing us deeper into the truth that we are not alone, unprotected, or uncared for when life gets complicated. Consider making a list of three concerns you are now willing to surrender, knowing what the Holy Spirit can do with a surrendered heart.

ADVENT PRAYER

Spirit of the living God,
hold me close
as I learn to lean
on the only one
who cannot lose
His grip.
Amen.

Holy Spirit Nudges
AT CHRISTMAS

———

The Holy Spirit is called our comforter. If you're looking to spend yourself in a spiritually enriching way this Advent, spread "tidings of *comfort* and joy." Many homeless shelters could use additional volunteers during the holidays, but they also need nonperishable comfort food like packets of premade hot cocoa or apple cider, personal hygiene gift sets, or donations of warm socks.

The First Twinges

While they were there [in Bethlehem], the time came for her to give birth.

Luke 2:6 AMP

Every woman "with child" carries internal dialogue—which often turns into conversations with other moms, her husband, friends at church—many waking and sleepless moments of the nine-month journey.

Boy or girl? Mary knew the answer to that one. *What will we name the child?* She knew that answer already, too. *What will my baby look like? Am I eating what the growing babe needs? What will labor be like? Or rather, what will my labor be like in comparison to all the stories I've heard—encouraging and discouraging?*

Mary knew she had the ear of the Holy Spirit. What kind of discussions did they have together?

If we flip ahead a few pages in our Bible, we find the distinct roles of the Holy Spirit match what someone like Mary would need. What someone like you and I need (emphases added).

- *Comforter*—"But the **Comforter**, which is the Holy Ghost, whom the Father will send in my name, he shall teach you all things, and bring all things to your remembrance, whatsoever I have said unto you" (John 14:26 KJV).

- *Wisdom*—"The Spirit of the LORD will rest on him— the Spirit of **wisdom** and of **understanding**, the Spirit of **counsel** and of **might**, the Spirit of the **knowledge** and **fear of the LORD**" (Isaiah 11:2).

- *Reminder*—"But when the Father sends the Advocate as my representative—that is, the Holy Spirit—he will teach you everything and will **remind you of every- thing I have told you**" (John 14:26 NLT).

- *Life Giver*—"Because through Christ Jesus the law of **the Spirit who gives life** has **set you free** from the law of sin and death" (Romans 8:2).

- *Peace-of-Mind Giver*—"The mind governed by the flesh is death, but the **mind governed by the Spirit is life and peace**" (Romans 8:6).

- *Explainer*—"The Spirit of wisdom and of **understanding**" (Isaiah 11:2). Note that almost every version of the Bible translates the Holy Spirit's role in this passage as "wisdom and understanding." It is because of the Holy Spirit that we can understand what might otherwise be hard to comprehend.
- *Helper*—"Likewise the Spirit also **helps** in our weaknesses" (Romans 8:26 NKJV).
- *Prayer Guide*—"We do not know what we ought to pray for, but **the Spirit himself intercedes for us** through wordless groans" (Romans 8:26).
- *Teacher*—"But the Helper, the Holy Spirit, whom the Father will send in My name, **He will teach you all things**, and bring to your remembrance all things that I said to you" (John 14:26 NKJV).
- *Advocate*—"But the **Advocate**, the Holy Spirit, whom the Father will send in my name, will **teach** you all things and will **remind** you of everything I have said to you" (John 14:26).
- *Power*—"But you will receive **power** when the Holy Spirit comes upon you" (Acts 1:8 NLT).

What comforts did the Comforter offer Mary? What assurances and reassurances did He whisper? What did He teach her that she needed to know if shunned by the community? How often did the Spirit remind her that she had been chosen—hand-picked—and that when God does the choosing, we don't need to spend a moment doubting our calling?

What wisdom did the Spirit offer regarding parenting a unique child, wisdom she no doubt collected as if creating a file for "How to Mother a Savior"?

Did she sing again the song (the Magnificat, Luke 1:46–55) the Holy Spirit gave her, practicing it as a lullaby? Did she ask the Spirit, "Will You tell me again that everything will be all right?" It's a question with which many of us are familiar.

Did she ask the Holy Spirit about the strange pains that gripped her? "Is this it? Is this labor? Is it time?"

Where was the Spirit when the labor intensified? He was there. Hovering. He may have nudged Joseph to place his fists in the small of her back to bring a measure of relief. The Spirit was breathing His sweet breath to cool her brow. Perhaps even pushing through the census-bloated Bethlehem crowd to find a place for them—a place utterly beautiful in its simplicity, seclusion, and rawness, what we would consider an imperfect place for a babe to be born, much less a King. Imperfect in our eyes only. But not God's plan B, C, or D. How much richer a story it is because the setting itself represented the awe that the Son of God would be sent among us to save us.

Humans would have wanted to speak into the stable situation. "Come on, somebody! Have a little sympathy. Can't you see the woman's about to have a baby?" They still entertain that debate.

The animals merely watched in wonder when the Spirit said, "Push. Push!"

The way God the Father had orchestrated everything leading to the moment of Jesus's birth still puts us in awe:

> Bible scholars have concluded from much research that, hundreds of years before Jesus was even born, more than 300 prophecies were recorded to tell of His coming, His life and journey to the cross, and the power of His Resurrection. These prophecies point to the exact location, circumstances, and even timing of Jesus Christ's birth.[1]

After no-one-knows-how-many hours of labor, the child slipped into the world. And nothing has been the same since. It was a pivotal moment in history, and a pivotal moment individually for those who would believe.

With the now six-month-old John's connection to the Spirit, don't you wonder if at the moment of Jesus's birth, the little boy stirred in his sleep, a subconscious-level smile on his infant face? Would Elizabeth have bent over baby John, noted the curious smile, and done the math?

"Nine months ago, Mary came to me. Was tonight the night the Savior was born?"

It's no stretch to consider that Elizabeth might have been praying for Mary even then.

If we were orchestrating the events, we would have had Jesus born at the Nazareth Medical Center, wrapped in a monogrammed baby blanket with family and friends waiting to hand out blue M&M's, and Mary's greatest concern being which infant photographer to use.

The birth of Jesus—everything about it—was unexpected from our perspective but planned to the smallest detail in eternity past in the heart of God.

No pristine, sterile hospital birthing center. A crude, messy, no-doubt smelly stable, and the manger may well have been made of reclaimed wood.

No fanfare or parade served as a welcoming committee. No comforts like a baby shower or a well-appointed nursery.

Messy. Uncomfortable. Uncertain—for everyone but God.

But that's exactly why Jesus came. Because the world—and we—are a mess without Him. We're the "before" in before-and-after pictures. Our souls are in need of restoration.

The promises of God tell us that Jesus came to restore joy, meaning, peace, relationships, focus, purpose, broken and bruised memories, calm, healing, fresh starts, wonder, and hope. Jesus came to restore *hope*.

If you're looking for the Holy Spirit in the Christmas story, look in the stable, too. His presence made a crude location become sacred and a common experience—the birth of a child—holy.

◆ PONDERINGS ◆

Of the attributes or roles of the Holy Spirit mentioned in these pages, which ones stir your heart most? Those can change depending on our current circumstances, but it's faith-building to ponder that what we need is what He offers. And what better time for pondering than now?

◆ ADVENT PRAYER ◆

As we celebrate the coming of the Son,
with gratitude to the Father,
may our love and appreciation
for You, the Spirit,
swell
and give birth
to increasing faith.
Amen.

Angel Lyrics

Suddenly a great company of the heavenly host appeared with the angel, praising God and saying, "Glory to God in the highest heaven, and on earth peace to those on whom his favor rests."

Luke 2:13–14

Some of us listen to the retelling of the Christmas story with less enthusiasm than it deserves. It's as if we're reciting words rather than being excited by them.

It's not a monotone story. It's not emotionless. It is Spirit-infused, and "where the Spirit of the Lord is, there is freedom" (2 Corinthians 3:17). Freedom to worship. Freedom to experience the story body, mind, soul, and spirit.

That was certainly true on the night ordinary shepherds were tending their flocks on an ordinary hillside when the Father, Son, and Holy Spirit decided, "Let's tell *them* first!"

Talk about a casting crisis! These are the people who first hear the news? They have no standing in the community, no voice in the crowd to influence others, no audience. But as we'll soon see, the world would hear through the shepherds, empowered by the Spirit, "That baby? He's the Son of God!"

What delight it must have given the Godhead to deliver such news to the least likely, socially speaking, culturally speaking, even religiously speaking. At that time, who were the people technically the *most* knowledgeable about God's laws? The priests and Pharisees. But these shepherds, minding their own business, with seemingly no influence, were entrusted with and gifted the wonder-news.

Who composed the lyrics to the angels' chorus? The Divine Inspirer.

Who gave the downbeat direction "Now!"?

Who lit the sky on fire when the glory of God was revealed, and who watched with delight as the hillsides rang with the news?

Instructed by the Spirit, the head angel said, "For unto you is born this day in the city of David a Saviour, which is Christ the Lord" (Luke 2:11 KJV).

A Savior—the answer to Eve's ancient prayer.

The city of David—a king's residence, predicted long ago.

The angel of the Lord told the shepherds—those chosen as first to hear the lullaby music that rings through hallways in a maternity ward—"A baby has been born!"

And the angel began with words with which we've become familiar in our journey through Advent, words that often started an angel's or the Holy Spirit's messages: "Don't be afraid."

We think we remember well the event of common shepherds first hearing the news. Listen to it afresh from the Passion Translation:

> That night, in a field near Bethlehem, shepherds were watching over their flocks. Suddenly, an angel of the Lord appeared in radiant splendor before them, lighting up the field with the blazing glory of God, and the shepherds were terrified! But the angel reassured them, saying, "Don't be afraid, for I have come to bring you good news, the most joyous news the world has ever heard! And it is for everyone everywhere! For today in Bethlehem a rescuer was born for you. He is the Lord YAHWEH, the Messiah. You will recognize him by this miraculous sign: You will find a baby wrapped in strips of cloth and lying in the feeding trough!" Then all at once in the night sky, a vast number of glorious angels appeared, the very armies of heaven! And they all praised God, singing: "Glory to God in the highest realms of heaven! For there is peace and a good hope given to the sons of men."
>
> Luke 2:8–14 TPT

Watching treasured Christmas movies may be among your family traditions. Some consider *A Charlie Brown Christmas* their favorite because, unexpectedly, it is the voice of a child who delivers the glorious news.

I don't think I'm the only one who tears up at that version—hearing the simplicity of a child's voice (an eight-year-old child actor named Christopher Shea playing Linus) announcing the birth of a life-changing, heart-changing, history-altering baby.

As we might imagine for a children's animated movie, executives behind the scenes wondered, even until a week before first airing in 1965, whether including a word-for-word Scripture passage might alienate viewers. Charles Schulz, the creator of the cartoon, insisted. Even a popular soft drink sponsor gave its blessing. The night it aired, fifteen million people watched, and it became an instant classic. The following year, it won a Peabody award and an Emmy for Outstanding Christmas Programming.[1]

Imagine for how many of those watching it might have been the first time they'd heard the true story of Jesus's birth! How many more than the initial fifteen million have viewed it since, in its entirety, no scenes cut?

Today that scene is still considered, as one producer noted, "the most magical two minutes in all of TV animation."[2]

Where is the Holy Spirit in the Christmas story? In the words and sweet voice of an animated Christmas special that is still airing after almost six decades and in the middle of a culture that claims it doesn't value biblical truth. If that doesn't put us in awe . . .

◆ PONDERINGS ◆

Find a video or audio version of the Luke 2:8–14 section of *A Charlie Brown Christmas* to view with your friends or family. This time, listen with your Holy Spirit "earbuds" turned up. You may find His familiar voice and His presence obvious in a child's rendition of the holy child's arrival.

◆ ADVENT PRAYER ◆

Thank You, Holy Spirit,
for making Your presence obvious
in extraordinary ways
to and through ordinary people.
May our hearts be "animated"
by the reality
that You are here,
among us,
still proclaiming the Good News!
Amen.

The Christmas Fruit of the Spirit

But the fruit produced by the Holy Spirit within you is divine love in all its varied expressions: joy that overflows, peace that subdues, patience that endures, kindness in action, a life full of virtue, faith that prevails, gentleness of heart, and strength of spirit.

Galatians 5:22–23 TPT

My husband will often come into the house and say, "Smells like supper."

Usually, he means that in a good way. Sometimes, though, he says it to indicate he noticed I was cooking Brussels sprouts or cabbage, or that I hid green peppers in something. He says he can't even tolerate the smell of an uncut green pepper in the refrigerator. Now, that's sensitive.

On the other hand, he also notices when I've been making peach cobbler, apple pie, or cinnamon coffee cake—a Christmas favorite.

We can walk through an apartment we'd like to rent or a home we're interested in purchasing and know in an instant that the previous owner or renter was a smoker or owned cats. I stepped into an elevator for a conference last year and was overcome with the smell of perfume, even though the conference in this high-end hotel was intentionally fragrance-free. The bellhop explained that a famous female pop star had a major concert at that hotel over the previous weekend. This was a Tuesday . . . and the overpowering fragrance of the concertgoers still lingered.

What does that have to do with Advent or the days after Christmas?

We've been searching for the presence of the Holy Spirit in the Christmas story and in our own stories. The Bible says it's easy to tell. Galatians 5:22–23 says that the peach cobbler of the Spirit—or rather, the fruit of the Spirit (the evidence of His presence in and around us)—is love, joy, peace, patience, kindness, goodness, faithfulness, gentleness, and self-control.

What does that look like specifically in light of our Advent preparations and Christmas?

Love—If the Holy Spirit is evident in our Christmas preparations and aftermath, love will be evident, too. We won't be motivated by gift-giving competition or obligation, but love flowing through us as we let the Holy Spirit have more and more of our being.

Joy—When the Holy Spirit is as obvious as the smell of warm cinnamon coffee cake in our lives, people watching us will see joy override worry or concern. Unrufflable joy. Joy that allows us to sing through tears sometimes.

Peace—Is Christmas chaotic in today's modern living? Usually. The genuine look of peace on our faces and the uncommon peace present in our homes speaks loudly of the Holy Spirit's presence and His power to maintain that peace.

Patience—If I act as if I cannot celebrate Christ's coming with my whole heart unless He answers the prayers that have been waiting in my prayer journal since last January, or the year before that, or the year before that, I am revealing the opposite of the presence of the Holy Spirit in my story. He helps me trust that answers are coming. And if the calendar page flips a few days after Christmas and they are still seemingly unanswered, I can still be at peace. If the table is missing a guest because someone I love is in rehab, the Holy Spirit within enables me to remain at peace. Insert your "reason not to have peace but you do anyway" here.

Kindness—Ask any checkout clerk during the holidays if kind customers stand out. I imagine some of them would even know that the fragrance they smell is perfectly ripe fruit of the Spirit.

Goodness—Many people are "good" during the holidays. Some of them for the right reasons. For others it's because of what it will net them. But goodness that permeates all days and doesn't disappear in holiday madness and reveals itself without drawing attention to itself is—to the aware—clearly the presence of the Holy Spirit.

Faithfulness—At Christmas, we can find faithfulness in where our attention is focused. The Bible tells us to walk in the Spirit, and that's spotlighted at a time when it's easy to choose our activities and reactions and attitudes by some other influence than the Spirit of God. Does Bible reading fall by the wayside in the weeks leading up to Christmas? Is that a Spirit-led Christmas? "So I say, walk by the Spirit, and you will not gratify the desires of the flesh. For the flesh desires what is contrary to the Spirit, and the Spirit what is contrary to the flesh. They are in conflict with each other" (Galatians 5:16–17).

Gentleness—Who would argue that we live in a world and culture that is often hostile? (And if you *do* argue that point, is that gentleness?) The Holy Spirit is known for doing things differently than the norm, as in visiting a virgin who would then bear the Son of God. Gentleness isn't common. In the pushing and shoving to get the last spiral-cut ham at the grocery store, look for the person who isn't pushing and shoving. That's most likely the one, the gentle one, who is letting the Holy Spirit live through her or him.

Self-control—What evidence is there of the Holy Spirit's presence in us regarding self-control at Christmas? Let's leave the buffet table "off the table" for the moment. Okay, we'll put it back on the list. What come to mind are the times we rely heavily on the Holy Spirit to help us hold our tongue before lashing out in irritation at whoever isn't helping. Does the Holy Spirit keep us from chiding the person—younger or older—who pops up with something totally inappropriate because that's who they are? Do we let the Holy Spirit provide us with better responses than the ones we were planning? But we might also see evidence in the lesser-seen or considered moments, like getting enough sleep and putting on the brakes before a relationship derails.

Have you considered where the Holy Spirit is in your Advent *you*? Your Christmas *you*? The *you* in the days after the Christmas thrill turns into cleanup and return to routine?

We know what the evidence looks and smells like. May this year's fruit smell a lot like cobbler.

◆ PONDERINGS ◆

Consider reading Galatians 5:22–23 as part of your new traditions for Advent. Note where the Holy Spirit shows up in the Christmas story and your story through His fruit.

◆ ADVENT PRAYER ◆

Holy Spirit,
we're not stepping
out of the Christmas story
to find You in our own.
We look to You to
grow in us
the evidence of Your presence
in our lives
and our anticipation.
Amen.

Holy Spirit Nudges
AT CHRISTMAS

—

This Advent season, consider how He may be prompting you to respond to the nudge to seek out a widow or widower, someone with a chronic medical condition, someone you haven't seen at church for too long, or an estranged family member. Offer a "thinking of you because Jesus is" card or small gift. Or simply—Holy Spirit–style—offer your presence.

And a New Star Is Born

"We observed his star rising in the sky and we've come to bow before him in worship."

Matthew 2:2 TPT

Astronomers who made it their business to observe the heavenly bodies couldn't believe what their eyes were telling them. A new star in the anciently same sky? They searched the scrolls in their libraries and long-told tales and found no answers to the phenomenon.

After much searching, they stumbled onto Hebrew prophecies that gave them the clues they needed. A star connected to a King. And they embarked on what was likely a many months-long journey to see that promised King for themselves.

Their Spirit-orchestrated research likely was what led them to consider, among other documents, the parchments and scrolls of the ancient Israelites. (As we recall from a timely census and the impact of Linus reciting Scripture in a Peanuts animation, the Holy Spirit can use anything and anyone!)

In the tablets and pages lay the only clue that made sense. From the age-worn texts, the astronomers made the connection that one of the Israelites, Daniel, had prophesied to their ancestors about this event when he was a captive in Babylon.

Because of Daniel's prophecy, they knew exactly who they were seeking and what they would find at the end of the star's journey. Daniel's faithfulness hundreds of years prior to speak what the Spirit of God had impressed upon him in a dream (see Daniel 7:13–14) now provided the astronomers with the answer as to why a new star had suddenly appeared. The One whose Kingdom could never be destroyed had been born!

Who else but the Spirit would have influenced them with "This is what all of creation has been waiting for. The Messiah. This is His star. If I were you, I'd follow it"?

After the Spirit visited Zechariah and Mary, they erupted in song. What might the astronomers' or wise men's song have sounded like?

> How many miles have we traveled?
> How many roads, how many grains of sand,
> How many other stars did we ignore
> As we followed the One?

The brightest
The One who appeared in a sky of what by contrast
Was inky dark, cave-dark, gem-stark
In the canopy above us.

We bore the jeers of those who questioned,
Why us? Why now? And how
Could anyone with a lick of sense,
Much less scientists or wisdom-seekers
Leave everything to follow one Star?

It wasn't a search for fame.
There are far easier ways to reach fame's status
Than choking on camel dust and sleeping to donkey
    brays
On a journey that seemed it would never end.

It wasn't a longing for significance.
Fanfare wasn't our pursuit.
What burned in our chests
And consumed our thoughts
Was a babe, a King
Who would make all other kings
Pale in His Light.

Who does that?

Who struggles with dust-hemmed robes of tapestry
And an ancient laundry list of gifts
In search of a baby's swaddle?
Who risks saddle sores and blistered feet

And the sun's cruel heat
To follow a young child's toddle?

Yet could we staunch the yearning?
Could we stop the burning
That day after cumbersome day drew us closer,
That night after glorious night reminded us
Of a Star shining and a Baby's birth,
And a King worth our everything?

No duty compelled us.
No country assigned us
The task.
We, like untold others
Who would walk this same path
Drew near
Because of the joy
Of discovery.

Joy that stole our breath
At the sight of Him.
Joy that soothed our souls
At the promise fulfilled.
Joy that thwarted another's evil intent.
Joy that changed us forever
Because we chose to follow
The One who is fullness of Joy.[1]

For much of my life, I assumed the wise men were smart guys. Or the three literal kings of "We Three Kings" fame. Nothing in

Scripture tells us specifically that there were only three or that they were royals, although the gifts they carried on their trip to honor this new King spoke of the wealth that might have been available to royalty.

Cultural history tells us they may have been more like scientists than they were political rulers, astronomers before the word was invented. They knew the night sky and knew it well. It was their primary focus of study.

Without the benefit of high-tech imaging and billion-dollar telescopes, they noticed a star that had not been charted before. And it did not move in sync with the rest of the known galaxy. A singularly unique star captured their attention and moved them.

Have you, too, assumed that the magi all worked in the same office somewhere out east of the Holy Land? Have you believed that they decided together to pursue that star, so they loaded their covered wagons with beef jerky and flatbread and cried out, "Westward ho!"?

Later historical documents suggest that those who followed the star were from three different regions in the East:[2]

Melchior from Persia

Gaspar from India

Balthazar from Arabia

Whether legend or historically accurate, how intriguing is it to think about the three guys (or thirty led by three) converging somewhere at the camel station and recognizing they were all following the same star.

One thing we know is that the Spirit of God touched those individuals with a longing to follow that star to find the King.

When they arrived in Jerusalem—less than six miles from their destination after a four- or five-month journey, they asked for an audience with King Herod. They asked the ruler, "Where is the one who has been born king of the Jews? We saw his star when it rose and have come to worship him" (Matthew 2:2).

They asked the king on his throne—a king with a vile and harsh reputation and wicked jealousy over his position, Herod— where they would find the *real* King who was *born* King of the Jews. Linger on that thought.

More precision lies in this beautiful report that only the biblical writer Matthew thought it important to report.

Matthew met Jesus during His earthly ministry and not only witnessed the coming of the Holy Spirit as a permanent resident of human hearts at Pentecost after Christ's return to the side of His Father, but was among those who first experienced the Holy Spirit not speaking from *without* but moving from *within* him.

Matthew ministered by the Spirit. He testified by the power of the Spirit. He wrote at the moving of the Spirit.

He, inspired by the Spirit, recorded the story of the magi who were motivated by the Spirit to follow a star that moved at the will of the Spirit. And Matthew's writings include details that connect other dots for us, which we'll soon see.

◆ PONDERINGS ◆

In your personal or family study times, when you see the words *Holy Spirit* or read of His work in individuals like Matthew, Mary, Zechariah, or the wise men, consider how you can flag those places. Use highlighting, a bookmark, or an asterisk as a reminder of the Spirit who now serves as our "remembrancer" (see John 14:26), calling to our minds the teaching of the child who became human and fulfilled His purpose by providing us with forgiveness of our sins, connection to the Father, and eternal life.

◆ ADVENT PRAYER ◆

Spirit of God,
I invite You to steer me
on my journey
to honor the King of kings
with my life.
Amen.

Rumor Has It

When they saw the star, they were overjoyed. On coming to the house, they saw the child with his mother Mary, and they bowed down and worshiped him.

Matthew 2:10–11

The wise men didn't discover *all* the prophecies about the star-king connection, or they would have known their eventual destination was Bethlehem, as foretold by Micah seven hundred years prior (see Micah 5:2–5). But they can be forgiven. The book of Micah is only seven chapters long. Easy to overlook. It wouldn't have made a very big scroll.

The astronomers journeyed as far as Jerusalem and thought to ask the one person they were sure would know where that

King would have been born—ruthless, vile, murderous, villainous King Herod.

Dudes!

On hearing the astronomers' question not about the validity of prophecy but about where they could *find* the one prophesied, Herod was "disturbed, and all Jerusalem with him" (Matthew 2:3).

Some other king? Two things must have rattled Herod. He had competition for his reign, and he did not know the answer to their question. Herod asked the teachers of the law where this supposed Messiah was to be born. They quoted from Micah 5 when they answered him. "Bethlehem."

The astronomers must have gone out for lunch while Herod consulted those who knew the prophecies, because he called them back secretly. Matthew 2:7 tells us he "found out from them the exact time the star had appeared."

An exact time. A precise moment the star first appeared.

When they told Herod the *when*, Herod directed them to Bethlehem, a mere six miles south of Jerusalem. He added, "Go and search carefully for the child. As soon as you find him, report to me, so that I too may go and worship him" (verse 8).

In the margin of my Bible, I wrote in capital letters: *LIE!*

Herod had no intention of worshiping some other king. History reports that he was what we would now describe as narcissistic and brutal. He didn't want to worship Jesus. He wanted to annihilate the child. And he trusted that the wise men would return to tell him exactly where to find the at that time likely eighteen-month-old or two-year-old boy.

He loved it when an evil plan came together.

But he hadn't counted on God's plan. Or the Holy Spirit's intervention.

The astronomers caught a glimpse of the star again when they left Herod. They followed the star until "it stopped over the place where the child was" (verse 9).

A specific place. Not Bethlehem in general. The star stopped over *the place*, the house, where the child and his parents were then living. Still in Bethlehem. Not Nazareth. From other verses and from historical reports, many biblical scholars believe that between the first appearance of the star, the astronomers' research, and the trek that likely took them several months, Jesus would have been a toddler, perhaps almost two years old, when the wise men arrived.

Two Greek words offer confirmation of that idea. When the shepherds visited, they found Jesus lying in a manger, and the word to describe Him was *brephos*, meaning "newborn or infant."[1] When the wise men visited, it's said they came to the *house* where Mary and Joseph were staying and laid their gifts before the *paidion*, meaning "little boy or young child."[2]

We're not given insight into why Mary and Joseph would have still been in Bethlehem, unless it was purely at the direction of the Holy Spirit. They may have remained in Bethlehem because they connected with relatives, or they wanted the child to be weaned before they took the long trip back to Nazareth. We may not know, but we can trust that Mary and Joseph moved at the will of the Spirit.

As did the wise men.

The Bible tells us that after their visit with the King of all kings, the boy whom they recognized as the fulfillment of ancient prophecies, the child they bowed to—as all will one day (see Philippians 2:10–11)—the astronomers were warned in a dream by none other than the Spirit to whom they had been listening.

They were warned not to return to Herod with the information that evil king had wanted them to gather. Convinced to listen to a Spirit they hadn't seen rather than to an earthly, power-grubbing king they had, they bypassed Jerusalem and returned to their homeland via another route (see Matthew 2:12).

The Spirit-driven star had not steered them wrong. They trusted the Spirit of the Lord. They didn't trust Herod. And rightfully so.

As soon as the wise men left, Joseph was warned in a similar Spirit-infused dream to take the child and His mother (interestingly, the child was mentioned first) and escape to Egypt. Yes, the same Egypt from which the children of Israel had fled so many years before this. It would now become their safe house. In the dream, Joseph clearly heard the why. "For Herod is going to search for the child to kill him" (verse 13).

How could Joseph trust a directive like that? Such upheaval of their lives and plans, of his work and their family connections.

Egypt must have seemed a very solitary place for them. He could trust the instruction because he recognized the voice of the Spirit of God.

Joseph might have assumed he could find safety in Nazareth in Galilee, that they could disappear and stay hidden from Herod. But he obeyed when the Spirit in essence said, "Not where you might assume. Not the answer you devise. Egypt."

Joseph was so intent on obedience to the voice of the Spirit that he got up in the middle of the night to escape to Egypt. They remained there until Herod died. But don't miss this detail. That action fulfilled yet another prophecy about Jesus. In Hosea 11:1 we read, "Out of Egypt I called my son."

Simple Christmas story? One of the most detailed and long-planned in history!

God cannot fail. He didn't this time, either. When Herod heard that he'd been outwitted by the smart guys, when the rumor reached his ears that the astronomers who were unknowingly drafted as spies had no intention of snitching on the location of the one *born* King of the Jews, he gave an order to eliminate all male children two and under in Bethlehem and the surrounding area. He calculated his order from the time the wise men told him they'd first seen the star.

The Spirit knew long before Herod spoke his sickening decree.

The Spirit spoke. Joseph obeyed. Jesus was protected.

◆ PONDERINGS ◆

Not everything about our Advent preparation time or the Christmas story is easy to consider. Herod's reaction to being usurped is horrific. Our Advent days may lead us to moments when, rather than celebration, we confess having ignored the Spirit's direction or taken guidance issues into our own hands rather than immediately obeying what God asks. How would life change if we would be like Joseph?

◆ ADVENT PRAYER ◆

Who among us, Lord,
would not need to confess
that we too often
are slow to hear
and sluggish to respond
to Your Spirit?
Speak, Spirit of God.
We're listening.
Amen.

Remodeling
Our Nativity Scenes

The shepherds returned, glorifying and praising God for all the things they had heard and seen, which were just as they had been told.

Luke 2:20

id you choose a traditional Christmas card this year, one with a silhouette of the city of Bethlehem—nothing moving, except perhaps three magi on camels plodding over the moonlit hillside with shepherds converging from the other direction . . . wise men who would not have begun their travels, we now know, until Jesus was no longer lying in a manger?

Peaceful setting, though, isn't it? Ancient Bethlehem. It's the stuff of ornaments and greeting cards and Nativity sets. But what was really happening in the country around the time Jesus appeared on the scene?

We're well aware by now that it had been four hundred years since God's people had heard from Him. They'd all chosen to do what was right in their own eyes (see Judges 17:6). Society was in utter chaos. Sound familiar?

The census-taking itself must have been chaos—the city of Bethlehem swelling with thousands of out-of-towners forced to travel there. Silent night? Not so much.

Jesus was born into a political firestorm that threatened the lives of babies like Him and sent waves of fear through their parents. Travel was hard and fraught with danger. Thieves abounded, as was mentioned—highway robbers as prevalent as cyber-highway robbers. The world at that time was writing the rules for racial tension. Family heartaches. Financial difficulties exacerbated by taxation. Homelessness. The world had been waiting for answers to prayer for thousands of years.

The same kind of chaos we see around us now.

The Christmas card picture doesn't show the armed guards, the fear, the hopelessness.

Many families have a dramatic story of a Nativity set gone wrong. The dog chewed the leg off the wooden donkey. An ember from the fireplace flared up and destroyed everything in the room except the Nativity set. The family's two-year-old hid

Baby Jesus in her pocket to "protect" him, but the Christ child took an amusement-park ride through the washer and dryer. The cardboard Nativity set from the 1950s somehow survived twelve military moves cross-country and back, but the metal strongbox of important papers didn't.

What's your Nativity set story? Steeped in family tradition? Great-grandma made it in ceramics class so you don't dare take it to the thrift shop? A kindergartner made it, puppet style, from felt and popsicle sticks, so you don't dare throw it out, even though the child's artistic skills have improved radically since then? Did you travel to the Holy Land or order an olive-wood set online? Are those teeth marks on the plastic sheep from your toddler, not your dog?

Does your Nativity set fit your memories but not your décor? Or the other way around? Is it more impressionistic or realistic? And how many Nativity sets truly are aligned well with what we know from the Bible?

What do we know for sure about the Nativity scene? The Holy Spirit was there.

Did the star *land* on the roof of the stable, as so many cardboard, plastic, ceramic, and wooden images portray? Let's visit Matthew 2:9 again. "They [the kings or wise men from the east] went on their way, and the star they had seen when it rose *went ahead of them* until it *stopped over the place* where the child was" (emphasis added).

They truly *followed* the star, moving where it moved. This navigation system to rival all navigation systems was reliable because the Spirit moved on the magi to assure them the star could be counted on and would be worth the journey.

The Spirit says the same to us.

A star overhead somehow pointed to a specific dwelling place. The atmosphere in the stable was real and gritty but chapel-like because of the presence of the Spirit changing the atmosphere.

No Nativity scene in art from ancient or modern times can capture the invisible presence of the Holy Spirit, who guided shepherds, directed the angelic host, made a stable enough, re-assured the magi they were on the right path with nothing but timeless writings, a cosmically curious star that moved against the sky, and the urging of their travel companion—the Spirit of God.

You won't see Him in the paintings or rearrange Him every year when you take the Nativity set out of storage. But He's there, orchestrating the details and breathing hope.

Consider this. In biblical times, a stable often wasn't a de-tached building. It was a hollowed area beneath the family dwelling. If that were the case, unlike most of the Nativity sets we've seen, Mary, Joseph, the baby Jesus, plus the invisible ob-server and comforter, the Holy Spirit, may have had a family living above them on that sacred night of Christ's birth. Is that in our Nativity sets? Imagine.

Imagine, too, how oblivious the owners must have been to the life-changing, world-changing, future-changing event hap-pening under their feet.

Was it a silent night? It was definitely a holy night.

The story behind the beloved Christmas hymn "Silent Night" is worth acknowledging. Search for the tale that suggests the words were first sung in a home with a gathering of friends like yours. Consider the wonder that this Christmas it will be sung in more than three hundred languages around the world. How does that reverberate in your heart?

How will you ensure that your family is not oblivious to or neglectful of the wonder of a Spirit-infused, sacred Christmas this year?

◆ PONDERINGS ◆

As Mary "treasured up all these things and pondered them in her heart" (see Luke 2:19), we are invited to consider.

What kind of conversations will you have with your family as you unbox and set up your Nativity set this season? How will the conversation be different when you include room for the Holy Spirit's presence?

◆ ADVENT PRAYER ◆

Immortal, invisible
Gentle Spirit,
reveal Your presence
where we see presents.
Speak to us
in the silence
or the chaos
of our gatherings.
May we acknowledge You
as profoundly
as if we
pulled another chair
to our holiday table.
Amen.

The Celebration

And the Spirit of holiness rested upon him. Simeon believed in the imminent appearing of the one called "The Refreshing of Israel."

Luke 2:25 TPT

*T*ime slip. The chronology of the Christmas story isn't told in a minute-by-minute, hour-by-hour fashion. Much of it is written in "meanwhile" style. We now slip back in time to when the astronomers were still consulting their navigation apps (*recalculating, recalculating*) in anticipation of eventually reaching the spot where the star was leading them, back in time to Jesus—at forty days old—who was carried to the temple in . . . wait for it . . . Jerusalem.

As was the custom, the child was taken to the temple in Jerusalem in compliance with Jewish tradition for what were called purification rites and was presented to Simeon. Note this. Herod hadn't heard about Jesus yet. Or he wasn't listening. Think of it, though. Perhaps as many as two years before Herod heard about this child, Jesus had already been to the temple in Herod's domain—Jerusalem.

Herod wasn't an issue yet for the young family. The only real challenge was the six-mile walk at forty days postpartum, the needs of a newborn, and finding a pair of doves or two young pigeons as a gift. I have a feeling the pigeons were the easy part.

Enter Simeon.

Why look at Simeon's story, which happened more than a month after Jesus's birth, during our Advent preparations? Because it's all connected. As you might guess, its connection is rooted in the Holy Spirit's presence and promise.

Simeon is described as righteous and devout. Luke 2:25 tells us he was "waiting for the consolation of Israel," or waiting for the Redeemer. What further is noted about Simeon? "The Holy Spirit was on him. It had been revealed to him by the Holy Spirit that he would not die before he had seen the Lord's Messiah. Moved by the Spirit, he went into the temple courts" (verses 25–27), just as Mary and Joseph brought Jesus to the temple.

If you've been marking references to the Holy Spirit in this story, those two verses alone may send you online to order more highlighters.

As Elizabeth had recognized the Messiah Mary carried within her, Simeon recognized the Messiah when he was laid in Simeon's arms for the ceremony. He then, you guessed it, broke into a song-like prayer, in essence saying, "I can now die a happy man."

He praised God, saying:

"Sovereign Lord, as you have promised, you may now dismiss your servant in peace. For my eyes have seen your salvation, which you have prepared in the sight of all nations: a light for revelation to the Gentiles, and the glory of your people Israel."

Luke 2:29–32

Does it strike you, too, that in this traditional Jewish ceremony, Simeon specifically mentioned Gentiles? The Holy Spirit was truly on him to prompt him—solidly entrenched in the teachings of the Torah—to proclaim these words that would not be fulfilled until decades later when Gentiles were invited to follow "the consolation of Israel," the Messiah.

Then Simeon addressed Mary. His words must have rocked her to the core. She had no doubt assumed her son, the Son of God, would stir controversy, that her road and His would not be easy, even this long before Herod's threats. But more became clear during the ceremonial blessing.

Simeon said, "This child is destined to cause the falling and rising of many in Israel, and to be a sign that will be spoken against, so that the thoughts of many hearts will be revealed. And a sword will pierce your own soul too" (Luke 2:34–35).

In that tenderest of moments with Mary, this baby dedication, Simeon—his spirit and mouth filled with words from the Holy Spirit—held the babe in his arms and spoke sympathetically, as if he knew Jesus and His mother were facing a difficult road. Why? Because Jesus was not an answer all would embrace. Coached by the Spirit of God, Simeon spoke of a time more than three decades into the future for the little one.

Other religious leaders didn't, but Simeon, with the Holy Spirit on him, recognized that the Good News of Jesus's arrival and His life's mission came at a high price—a price Mary, too, would pay in grief. It's a cradle-cross-crown moment. The small, Middle Eastern–skinned, eight-pound (or so) infant faced a journey from cradle to crown, with a cross between.

The Holy Spirit, the remembrancer, must have spoken into Simeon's soul the prophecies from ancient days—how the Savior would suffer and be pierced (see Psalm 22:17). Simeon looked into the eyes of the new mother and with great compassion related that she, too, would be pierced, as any mother's heart would be at the foot of the cross on which Jesus gave His life for our salvation.

Enter onto the scene another woman. While Mary and Joseph were at the temple for the purification and dedication ceremony, a woman from the tribe of Asher, the daughter of Penuel (who both have their own stories in Scripture), walked in on the family. The Bible describes her as "very old." She'd been married for seven years, then had lived as a widow for eighty-four years, which would make her likely more than one hundred years old, although some translations believe the wording to mean she was currently eighty-four. Either way, she'd been alive a long, long time.

But who was she? Anna was a woman who we're told "never left the temple but worshiped night and day, fasting and praying" (Luke 2:37). That kind of devotion and openness to the things of God made her so sensitive to the voice of the Holy Spirit that she recognized the forty-day-old infant as her Messiah.

"Coming up to them at that very moment, she gave thanks to God and spoke about the child to all who were looking forward to the redemption of Jerusalem" (verse 38).

Her specific words aren't recorded for us. But she knew. By God's grace and the ever-present-in-the-story Holy Spirit, she knew that the infant was the chosen One, the holy One, the Redeemer. And she lived the rest of her life changed—from spending her days worshiping the God who promised to send a Redeemer to praising the God who *had*! And telling everyone who would listen.

Three short verses record her life and accomplishments, the greatest of which was accomplished when she was "very old"—telling everyone she knew that the Savior had been born.

◆ PONDERINGS ◆

We've seen age (too young or too old), infertility, muteness, station in life, distance, saboteurs, impossibilities, and a babe who could not yet speak were not hindrances for a God who considers nothing impossible, whose timing is impeccable, and who is as concerned about minute details now as He ever was.

As you consider Simeon's and Anna's roles in the Advent and post-Advent scenes, are you encouraged that, empowered by the Holy Spirit, nothing stands in your way for expressing this most holy, most moving, most remarkable news?

You have a role in the story, too. Tell everyone within your reach that a Savior is within *their* reach.

◆ ADVENT PRAYER ◆

On this eve
that is noted throughout history
as a date
worth respecting
and the birth of a Son
worth worshiping,
may our overcoming thoughts
be wonder
and gratitude,

ignited by the Holy Spirit,
and uncontainable joy,
that the story
is for us.
Amen.

Holy Spirit Nudges
AT CHRISTMAS

This Advent season, consider how the Spirit may be prompting you to step out as Anna did. Reach out to those older than you and offer the gift of an hour of conversation, your attention, and sharing the Christmas story with them. You can rejoice together, or you may find someone who has yet to hear that the Savior has been born.

The Christmas "Others"

Jesus did countless things that I [John] haven't included here. And if every one of his works were written down and described one by one, I suppose that the world itself wouldn't have enough room to contain the books that would have to be written!

John 21:25 TPT

Just as we have sometimes overlooked the Spirit woven throughout the Christmas story and the Advent season—starting in the book of Genesis with the Spirit brooding over the unformed world that would so desperately need a Savior—we often overlook others in the story, many of them unmentioned in Scripture.

Who was the weaver who wove the swaddling clothes, likely unaware of the holy child whose body they would embrace?

We don't know. And we have likewise no idea if that weaver's family would have made the linen cloths that wrapped Christ's broken body for burial thirty-three years later. But knowing the intimate and intricate details involved in this ancient but ever-new story, it wouldn't surprise us, would it?

We assume an innkeeper rejected the young couple, Joseph and uber-pregnant Mary. Scripture tells us only that there was no room in the inn, not that an innkeeper crossed his arms or stomped his feet and said, "No admittance!"

But if he had, would the innkeeper's wife have snuck food to the new mom? And when the shepherds showed up, would the innkeeper have had a change of heart over the baby and have allowed the slack-jawed, baby-admiring shepherds on his property?

Surely someone—some long-lost relative of Joseph—would have taken the young family in for the duration of the census-taking and until the mother and babe were recovered enough to travel the ninety miles back to Nazareth, even before that plan was diverted by a Spirit-directed secretive escape to Egypt. Mary already knew what it was like to be a long-term house guest from her stay with Elizabeth and Zechariah. She'd only been in residence at Joseph's home for a few months. And now displaced again, temporarily, how she must have longed for her own nest. Her own cook fire, her own rooms and breathing space, her own garden, her own routine settling in with her new husband and the baby.

Who took them in? Scripture doesn't tell us.

As we've seen, God is a God of details. But some of those particulars He is apparently holding on to now so that He can delight us with them later.

Just as we're beginning to realize that so many unnamed others were affected by the birth, including generation after generation of people like us, we've also come to realize that the Spirit of God isn't always named in the story details. But we can be assured He was there.

Were there babies in *other* mamas' wombs that night who leaped or kicked or fluttered for the first time because they knew—if the sweet voice of the Spirit informed them—that something unusual had just happened in Bethlehem?

Think of all the unnamed who were camping out in and around Bethlehem who had also come from many miles for the census. After hearing about the remarkable birth—we know word would have gotten around since the shepherds were a chatty bunch—would those travelers have entertained doubts about their doubts?

"Could it be true? Could this child be the Messiah? No! Of course not. But what if?"

Who breathed the "what if" into them?

Who but the Holy Spirit would have lit a fire that burned in the hearts of those who had long been waiting for the Redeemer?

Who but the Holy Spirit could have quieted the new dad's fears about Herod's threats?

Who indeed but the Holy Spirit—there at the beginning, moving the hands of the scribes of old, speaking to prophets in their dreams, and "coming upon" a young chosen girl to accomplish something that had never been done before.

Who but the Holy Spirit would be a more trustworthy witness to the joy of that incomparable night?

And how can we, who have caught a glimpse of the Holy Spirit's presence, do anything but respond in awe and wonder?

◆ PONDERINGS ◆

As we've searched for evidence of the Holy Spirit's presence, there may be a scene or two that gripped your heart more profoundly than others. Which one was it? Knowing that He was there on the pages, in the room, how will it change your celebration and your heart in the days ahead?

◆ ADVENT PRAYER ◆

We thought we knew
joy.
We thought we knew
peace.
We thought we knew
comfort.
We thought we knew
reverence, wonder, worship.

Jesus, Savior of the world
And Savior of our souls,
thank You
for revealing even more
of the Father-heart of God
through the
constant,
unmistakable
presence
of the Holy Spirit
this Christmas season
and on and on and on . . .
amen. And amen.

ADDITIONAL RESOURCES

For Day 2:

Links to versions of Handel's Messiah

Using ancient instruments of Handel's day—https://www
.youtube.com/watch?v=r8mshjnAe3U

With lyrics—nothing but Scripture—https://www.youtube
.com/watch?v=CHK8hJ22SPw

Boys' choir in a cathedral—https://www.youtube.com
/watch?v=LFBIJgkj_-g

For Day 4:

Enjoy this version of "O Little Town of Bethlehem."
https://www.youtube.com/watch?v=Bx3KO0nYBMM

Ten Family Christmas Activities That Make Room for the Spirit

- **Determine to listen well.** We might wonder if Mary, Zechariah, the shepherds, or the astronomers would have heard if they hadn't been paying attention or if they had been consumed with other business or busyness. If you can—personally or as a family—set aside even a few minutes of time to listen intently, it's likely you'll hear Him speak in the depths of your heart. What if a Christmas *activity* was zero activity other than listening for His voice?

- **When you hear Christmas music in your home, on the car radio, in stores,** do you ignore it, or do you think about and discuss it? Consider spotlighting a different Christmas carol each day for a week, or one each week of Advent, and diving deeper into the lyrics, the story behind the story, and helping young family members understand the context of less-familiar wording.

- **Create a new tradition.** Some old traditions spotlight the pain of uncomfortable memories and may need to be reworked to become something new. If it is not the same without Grandpa reading the Christmas story, what if the new tradition became hearing the story through the sweet voice of the youngest reader in the family?

The Father sent the Son to give us a new story to tell, one the Holy Spirit empowers us to communicate. But Uncle Fred refuses to attend the family Christmas? Pray for restoration, but pass the potatoes.

What might be an important but previously painful or uncomfortable Christmas memory that you can reclaim from the rubbish heap and watch God turn into this year's restoration project for your family?

After my father died, we adult children decided to offer others the kind of generosity Dad offered to us, a reflection of our generous God. We collect money for a charitable project every year, one that he would have been drawn to, and we give a gift in his name.

In his honor, we sent financial Christmas gifts from that fund to help feed starving children, to a ministry for injured military personnel, to a Bible distribution project for the incarcerated, to a family radio ministry, and one year, we found the Korean orphanage where he'd spent Christmas Eve in a Marine uniform and sent a gift there.

The new tradition eased the pain of his loss and kept our attention focused on staying attentive for where the Spirit might lead us to give generously the following year.

What creative idea will your family carry out that will be meaningful to you and a blessing to others?

- **When making room for the Spirit, we usually must slide something else out of the way.** What are you and your family willing to set aside so you can honor the presence of the Holy Spirit this Advent season? Is it screen time? Excessive devotion to something that draws your attention away from Him rather than toward Him?

- **Turn off notifications.** What? Impossible! Or is it? What might happen if you agreed to turn off email, social media, and text message notifications for a time expressly to keep that tug, even subconscious sometimes, from distracting you from the "ding" the Holy Spirit may want to send?

- **Each day of Advent, post the Scripture from that day's Advent reading in this book on your desktop, a bathroom mirror, or your water bottle.** Repeat it often throughout the day, and revisit it before moving on to the next day's Scripture verse.

- **Illustrate your thoughts.** Even if you or your family don't consider yourselves artists, on paper or a with digital drawing program (or even stacked building blocks) create an image of what one of the scenes we walked through in this Advent devotional might have looked like. It can be as simple (Zechariah's writing implement) or complex (stable or temple scene) as you'd like. There's something about using a creative outlet to visually or kinesthetically engage with the concept that cements it in our brains.

- **Take turns reading the Christmas story in Luke 2:1–20** from a different version of Bible. If you only own one or two versions, check online for others, taking special note of differences that throw new light on that familiar-to-many passage.

- **Host a movie marathon night** with popcorn and Christmas movies that honor the real story of Christmas, or even if the real story isn't spelled out, point out the moments that are reflections of how the Holy Spirit moves (special messenger, generosity, comfort, peace, caring, counseling, protecting, guiding). Invite a friend or your children's friends.

- **Few people—some say too few—send Christmas cards these days.** If sending to all your friends and family feels daunting, make room for the Spirit to compel you to write to the one person He suggests you connect with this Christmas. Spend time writing down thoughts that will uplift and encourage. Sign it with words like: *Because of the love of God, the gift of Jesus, and the power of the Holy Spirit, may your Christmas be especially blessed.* Then sit for a moment in quietness. Is there another person He might bring to mind?

ADDITIONAL ADVENT ACTIVITIES FOR YOU AND OTHERS

The Bible Project—Purchase a simple Bible, an inexpensive one if you choose, and as you read it, highlight all references to the Spirit of the Lord, the Spirit of God, the Holy Spirit. Take special note of Jesus's loving promise to send the Holy Spirit for His followers. On days when you wonder where He is in your situation, fan through the Bible and notice the Spirit's presence on the pages of Scripture as well as on the pages of your own story.

Consider marking two Bibles at once in this way—one for you, and one for a friend or family member in need.

The Christmas Bible Project—Do the same with a Bible in which you underline or highlight references to the role of the Holy Spirit in verses that foretell the coming of Christ or, in the New Testament, that record the events surrounding Christ's birth. That Bible might be one you pull out and leave on display at Christmas with all the other evidence that you are celebrating.

THE SPIRIT OF CHRISTMAS FOR YOU

Advent Is Action

Read Luke 1:47–55.

Christmas and restoration. They're synonymous in so many ways.

What we know about the need for Jesus coming to earth is first noted with the Spirit of God hovering over a yet unformed earth that would be peopled by humans who would choose disobedience over obedience and create a desperate need for a Redeemer. A restoration expert.

Jesus came to restore the relationship with God that hadn't been possible since sin entered the world. The gift of God's Son restored hope for mankind. Jesus coming in human form restored our faith in God's indescribable, unfailing-no-matter-how-long-it-takes love.

And the Holy Spirit lives within that story, and within our story, to remind us His love never fails.

Do some Christmas memories bite into your soul like the springs of a chair in need of restoration might poke and cut and jab?

- An uncle refuses to come to the holiday celebration if his brother will be there.
- A grandparent's obvious inequality in gift giving for a favored grandchild sends a wave of discomfort through the whole family—oldest to youngest—every year.
- Christmas celebrating has lost its luster in light of the medical crisis the family is facing.
- The memories won't be the same in the assisted-living center that now substitutes for the family home that once served as the gathering spot.
- Unforgiveness is an unwelcome guest at every holiday meal.
- We can only imagine how Christmas festivities with a sweet babe in a manger would feel to a couple who has lost a child that year.
- Or how offensive Christmas lights might feel to someone whose world is darkened with depression.
- Or how television commercials about loving families gathered around a feast spread on the table before them

would feel to a person without a family or food or shelter, or whose family is estranged or bickering or missing a loved one.

Do any of the above situations describe your upcoming Christmas?

Many of us don't approach Christmas with uninterrupted joy and unshadowed peace, with excitement and anticipation and an overflow of love.

And that, too, is where the Holy Spirit shows up in the story.

The Father sent the Son to be the restorer of relationships. And He sent the Holy Spirit to remind us of that.

All around us are the broken, worn-out, run-down, in need of repair, gouged by life's injustices and injuries, faded, unprotected, uncared for, missing something vital. . . .

As I read the Christmas story again recently, I noted the action in the prophet Zechariah's perspective about the coming Messiah—Jesus. He blessed God for sending Jesus, whom he knew was mere months away from being born. In Zechariah's blessing, he referred to God's *activity*, not merely theological concepts (see Luke 1:68–75). He listed, among others, these action words on God's part:

He **comes** to **help,** and He **delivers** His people.
He **raised** up a mighty Savior.

He **brought** salvation from our enemies and from the
   power of all those who hate us.

He **shows** the mercy promised.

He **rescues** from the power of our enemies.

Mary's song of praise that we heard when she was explaining
to Elizabeth that she'd been tasked with carrying the Messiah
in her womb (see Luke 1:47–55) includes these action words:

He **scatters** those with arrogant thoughts and proud
   inclinations.

He **pulls** the powerful down from their thrones.

He **lifts** up the lowly.

He **fills** the hungry with good things.

He **comes** to the aid of His servant.

And why? It's an epiphany for many of us. Why did God *act*
by sending Jesus? Why did God offer Jesus as our restoration?

"So that we could serve him without fear, in holiness and
righteousness in God's eyes, for as long as we live" (Luke 1:74–75
CEB).

The world had waited so long for a redeemer. Until Christ
was born, hope was a promise, but it was also an intangible.

We humans have always had trouble with intangibles in our
relationships.

Show me you love me.

Show me you're sorry for what you did.

Show me I can trust you.

Show me you care.

It's been the same in our relationship with God. We listen to His words, hear His stories, and understand His truths. But the arrival of Jesus on the scene was, in a way, God's response to a world that cries out, "Show me!"

Hope was born in a tangible, active way at Christmas.

Hope is one of the deepest longings of the human heart. Without it, our souls shrivel and gasp for breath.

Jesus's birth proved once again that God keeps His promises—all of His promises. Hope soars when we grasp that concept.

Life can be hard, harsh, and hurtful and still be hope-hemmed.

The Holy Spirit has always been in the business of restoring, reclaiming, refurbishing, renewing, and recycling.

Christmas is one of His display rooms of that concept.

Broken world? God knows, and He takes the scraps and salvaged pieces to make us sit up and take notice of a baby who has flawless skin and a flawless heart and who changes everything and offers us the opportunity to redeem disappointments into action-adventures. He helps us find joy and hope again in unexpected places.

The Christmas story we've come to embrace and honor isn't rooted in applauding winter or venerating a generous St. Nicholas. Its foundation is a historic moment—when God became man and dwelt among us. Immanuel dwelt among us. It's *imprinted on our restored hearts.*

Our generous, love-motivated God sent His Son to rescue and redeem, to bring light, life, and restoration. Jesus came in an unexpected way to an unsuspecting people, wrapped in inexpressible hope.

◆ PONDERINGS ◆

Read through Romans 15:13 slowly, noting the presence of the Father, Son, and Holy Spirit and the action-based promises of giving, providing, enabling, infusing, and filling that reflect what mirrors our Advent and Christmas longings. Choose an action that reflects the Holy Spirit as you give, provide, and fill someone with joy this week.

◆ PRAYER ◆

*Our gratitude rings loud and strong
for You, Holy Spirit,
as we move forward
in Your power
to bless others
as You have blessed us.
May we never lose sight
of where You are,*

where You're working,
and how near
You've chosen
to remain with us.
Amen.

ACKNOWLEDGMENTS

It has been a deep honor to accompany you through the Advent season by way of the pages of this book. Yes, I've been walking through the pages with you and praying that your appreciation for and awareness of the presence of the Holy Spirit in the Christmas story made a difference for you and your family as it did for me.

I've been writing professionally since Noah's children were babies, it seems. Scripts for a radio ministry eventually led to novels and nonfiction that now bow and bend my bookshelves. Almost fifty titles to date, including compilations, other devotionals, and even character sketches and sidebars in two different Bible projects.

Creating this Advent journey is among the highlights of my writing career because of the way it began—a shouted conversation across a noisy conference breakfast table that eventually became a proposal and then a contract—and because of what the Holy Spirit accomplished within me as I dug into "Where is the Holy Spirit in the Christmas story?"

When tasked with writing an Advent book about discovering the Holy Spirit in the Christmas story, I was excited for the challenge and the personal journey. But I had no idea how fortifying it would be for my faith. I see this book as an experience rather than mere words or encouragement. My prayer is that it invites readers, as it did me, to not only *watch for* but *marvel at* the Holy Spirit's role in this traditionally Jesus-centered story.

The process solidified for me not only the magnificence of the triune God we serve but the indispensable purpose of the Holy Spirit and His inescapable presence.

My husband often heard "Oh, honey! Listen to this about Simeon!" or similar comments as I wrote. My own heart heard "This. This is what you have too often overlooked in your quick read-through or your assumptions about a story you've heard so often that you think you have it memorized."

I may have had the words, but I had not always noticed the nuance. And the nuance is often where the Spirit hangs out.

Thank you, editor Kim Bangs and the Chosen/Baker Publishing Group team, for the gift of this assignment. I am forever changed. And thank you, Lori Janke and Hannah Ahlfield, for your attention to the project and your personal encouragement.

Janet Grant and the rest of the Books & Such Literary Management team, by now you know just how deep and genuine is my appreciation for all you do.

Reader, if you'd like to connect with me—for other books I've had the privilege to write, for additional companion ideas, for Christmas novels to enhance your holiday reading and your faith walk through this sacred season, or to schedule speaking events for women's retreats or gatherings, such as a Christmas tea for women—you can reach me in any of these ways:

CynthiaRuchti.com/Contact
HemmedInHope.com
Facebook.com/CynthiaRuchtiReaderPage
Instagram.com/CynthiaRuchtiAuthor

Thank you, readers, for exploring and discovering anew—or for the first time—the power, purpose, and soul-stirring presence of the Holy Spirit in the Christmas story.

As you know by now, this isn't your average Advent devotional. I pray it expressed the truth the Holy Spirit has been waiting for someone to talk about.

NOTES

Day 2 Isaiah's Conversation with the Spirit

1. Consider taking time to listen to an online recording of this segment of Handel's *Messiah* before reading on. You can find links in the Additional Resources page at the end of this book.

Day 3 Immanuel, God with Us . . . God Within Us

1. Danielle Bernock, "Is It Emmanuel or Immanuel?" Christianity.com, December 13, 2024, https://www.christianity.com/wiki/holidays/is-it-immanuel-or-emmanuel-biblical-meaning-and-significance.html.

Day 4 O Significant Town of Bethlehem

1. "1035. Beth Lechem," BibleHub.com, 2025, https://biblehub.com/hebrew/1035.htm.

Day 7 The Night Visitor

1. "Episkiazō," BlueLetterBible.org, 2025, https://www.blueletterbible.org/lexicon/g1982/kjv/tr/0-1/.

2. One of the times "overshadowed" (*episkiazō*) is used in the Bible is at the baptism of Jesus by John. Expressed in Mark 9:7 (NLT), "Then a cloud overshadowed them, and a voice from the cloud said, 'This is my dearly loved Son. Listen to him.'"

Day 9 The Glorious Turning

1. Vigdis Hocken and Konstantin Bikos, "Common Era (CE) and Before Common Era (BCE)," TimeAndDate, https://www.timeanddate.com/calendar/ce-bce-what-do-they-mean.html.

2. Cynthia Ruchti (inspired by the hymn "Turn Your Eyes upon Jesus," Helen H. Lemmel, 1922, Public Domain), © 2024.

Day 17 Mary's Nesting Months

1. Joel Ryan, "Advent Wreath: Meaning, Symbolism, Purpose of Advent Candles," Christianity.com, December 23, 2024, https://www.christianity.com/wiki/holidays/advent-wreath-meaning-of-advent-candles.html.

Day 18 The First Twinges

1. Debbie McDaniel, "Bible Verses That Prophesy Jesus Christ's Birth," Crosswalk.com, December 16, 2024, https://www.crosswalk.com/special-coverage/christmas-and-advent/10-bible-verses-that-prophesy-christ-s-birth.html#google_vignette.

Day 19 Angel Lyrics

1. Ken Zurski, "The Most Magical 'Two Minutes' in TV Animation," UnrememberedHistory.com, December 19, 2017, https://unrememberedhistory.com/tag/luke-2-8-14/.

2. Zurski, "The Most Magical 'Two Minutes' in TV Animation."

Day 21 And a New Star Is Born

1. Poem written by Cynthia Ruchti, 2023.

2. Jean-Pierre Isbouts, "Who Were the Three Kings in the Christmas Story?" NationalGeographic.com, December 24, 2018, https://www.nationalgeographic.com/culture/article/three-kings-magi-epiphany.

Day 22 Rumor Has It

1. "1025. Brephos," BibleHub.com, 2025, https://biblehub.com/greek/1025.htm.

2. "3813. Paidion," BibleHub.com, 2025, https://biblehub.com/greek/3813.htm.

CYNTHIA RUCHTI

is the author of almost fifty books and tells stories hemmed-in-Hope. She draws from real life and real faith, a deep heart for God and His Word, and past experiences writing and producing "The Heartbeat of the Home" radio broadcast. Her books have been recognized by RT Reviewers' Choice Book of the Year, PW Starred Reviews, Christian Retailing Awards, Readers' Choice Awards, the Carol Award, two Christy finalists, and more. Her tagline—"I can't unravel. I'm hemmed in Hope"—describes both what she writes and how she seeks to live. Cynthia and her husband make their home in the heart of Wisconsin.

CONNECT WITH CYNTHIA

CynthiaRuchti.com
HemmedInHope.com

@Cynthia.Ruchti or
@CynthiaRuchtiReaderPage

@CynthiaRuchtiAuthor

@CynthiaRuchti